EDUCATIONAL COMPLEX IN THE DISCIPLINE 'PHILOSOPHY' FOR STUDENTS WITH RUSSIAN LANGUAGE OF INSTRUCTION

G.A. TOKHTASUNOVA

F. YULDASHEVA

Educational complex in the discipline 'Philosophy' for students with Russian language of instruction
by: G.A. Tokhtasunova / F. Yuldasheva
Edition: January '2024
Publisher:
Taemeer Publications LLC (Michigan, USA / Hyderabad, India)

ISBN 978-93-5872-380-9

Book	:	Educational complex in the discipline 'Philosophy' for students with Russian language of instruction
Author	:	G.A. Tokhtasunova / F. Yuldasheva
Publisher	:	Taemeer Publications
Year	:	'2024
Pages	:	126
Title Design	:	*Taemeer Web Design*

INTRODUCTION

"Teachers perform a very important historical mission" - President of Uzbekistan Sh.M. Mirziyoyev.

The teacher is today a key figure in the entire education system of the Republic of Uzbekistan. The discipline "General Philosophy" refers to the general humanitarian and socio-economic cycle of disciplines for the professional training of students in their specialty. The professionalism of a teacher is the support and factor that will determine the success of ongoing reforms in the field of Education. The proposed modules for sections of the "Philosophy" course are developed on the basis of the State educational standard for general philosophical training. Education is presented as the most important sphere of spiritual activity. The discipline "Philosophy" is aimed at developing general competence to plan and implement one's own professional and personal development. The content of the discipline covers a range of issues related to ideological aspects of resolving the issue of the world as a whole, the place of man in this world, the meaning of life and the purpose of man, philosophical problems of nature and society, knowledge of the laws of natural and social reality, reflection of the historical and philosophical heritage. It is the basis, the theoretical core of the worldview and the general methodology of cognition and activity. Philosophy is not a set of facts, names, information that you just need to know and be able to reproduce (although it is also desirable to do this). As a result of studying philosophy, not only a person's thesaurus changes, but he himself changes. His worldview and attitude acquire harmony, systematicity, and integrity.

In the process of comprehending world philosophical thought, getting acquainted with its thousand-year amazingly interesting history, one can find and discover such a thinker, school, movement of philosophy, whose views on life, man, and the world as a whole would meet the challenges and demands of our time.

Compiled by:	G.A. Tokhtasunova lecturer at the Department of Social Sciences and Humanities, Pedagogy and Psychology, ASIYA
Reviewers:	F.Yuldasheva Doctor of Philosophy, Professor, Head of the Department of Philosophy, ADU
	T. Ortikov Doctor of Philosophy, Professor of the Department of Philosophy at ADU

TOPIC 1: MAIN GOALS OF PHILOSOPHY THEORETICAL AND PRACTICAL IMPORTANCE OF TEACHING IT TO FUTURE TEACHERS.

Key words: philosophy, purpose of philosophy, functions of philosophy, types of ancient philosophy.

The main goals of philosophy are the theoretical and practical significance of teaching it to future teachers.

Philosophy is a field of knowledge that deals with fundamental questions about the nature of existence, the goals and meaning of life, knowledge, morality and other aspects of existence. The main goals of philosophy may vary depending on the specific direction or movement, but common features include the search for truth, understanding the basic laws of the world, and the study of the principles of thinking and cognition.

The theoretical significance of teaching philosophy to future teachers is to help them develop critical thinking, analytical skills and the ability to systematize knowledge. Philosophy can provide teacher education students with a theoretical foundation for understanding different educational approaches, ethical issues, and fundamental principles of teaching.

Practical value includes the ability to apply philosophical principles in real life and in the learning process. Future teachers, studying philosophy, can develop their own pedagogical philosophy, which will serve as the basis for decision-making in the educational process, educational work and interaction with students.

Teaching philosophy to educators helps them think meaningfully about educational issues, develop their own vision of educational goals and values, and become deeper thinkers who are able to analyze and solve complex problems in education.

Discussion about the teaching of philosophy in this context involves the participation of various participants representing different aspects of education and philosophy. Let's look at the main points and questions raised in this conversation.

The need for new teaching staff and modern technical education

The introduction to the discussion begins with questions about the possibility of making a breakthrough in the country's development in economic, technological and social terms without new teaching staff and modern technical education. Obviously, such progress requires new approaches to education and training, and therefore the training of appropriate teachers is important.

Teaching philosophy in pedagogical universities

The specifics of teaching philosophy in pedagogical universities are considered. It is argued that existing programs differ little from the programs of other universities. It is noted that philosophy is often viewed as an additional burden that has no obvious applied significance. Programs are formed based on templates, without deep analysis, which reduces their effectiveness.

Problems in competency formulations

The problem of formulating competencies in programs is discussed. It is noted that even if the formulations are correct, they are not considered as a key element in the formation of philosophical education. Teachers often adapt them mechanically, without in-depth understanding.

Requirements for "paper" support of the educational process

It is indicated that regulatory documents impose strict requirements for "paper" support of the educational process, which can create obstacles to the introduction of changes and innovative approaches to education.

Overall, the discussion highlights the shortcomings of existing philosophy teaching programs in pedagogical universities and raises doubts about their effectiveness in training personnel capable of coping with the challenges of our time.

It also raises a number of important issues related to the development and teaching of philosophy programs in Russian universities. Here are a few key points:

1. Standardization of programs:

It is argued that work programs are often created using standard templates and do not take into account the specifics of the university or specialty. This may limit flexibility in teaching and may not take into account the individual characteristics of students.

2. Lack of attention to teaching methods:

It is noted that little attention is paid to teaching methods. Teachers, especially the older generation, may have a good command of the material, but do not always use modern teaching methods, which can hinder the effectiveness of the educational process.

3. The gap between the declared program and real work with students:

It is noted that often real work with students does not correspond to the declared programs. Sometimes teachers are forced to deviate from approved programs due to enthusiasm and creativity, which can be both a positive and negative aspect.

Problems with building a teaching system

The question arises about how effectively the teaching system can be built. It is argued that all attempts in this direction are made exclusively by enthusiasts, which can lead to inconsistency and lack of structure in the educational process.

Experience in secondary school and secondary specialized education

It is indicated that some successful methodological developments are found in secondary school and secondary specialized education, especially within the framework of the social science module “Social Studies”. Such approaches can provide useful experience for improving the teaching of philosophy in universities.

This can highlight the problems of standardization, lack of attention to methodology, the gap between stated programs and real practice, as well as the need for a systematic approach to teaching philosophy.

The presented text raises problems related to the teaching of philosophy in universities and the formalization of the educational process. Here are the main aspects:

1. Paper creation and formalization:

University teachers are faced with excessive paperwork and formalization of their activities. This creates difficulties in discussing and solving real problems, as well as in developing new teaching methods and technologies.

2. The gap between the formality of programs and real activities:

The programs indicate that philosophy is a means of developing thinking and intellectual competencies, but the structure of the course and the organization of educational activities do not allow these goals to be realized. There is a gap between the formality of educational programs and real work with students.

3. Lack of a unified position regarding the modern function of philosophy:

Universities do not have a common position on what function philosophy should perform in education and culture. This leads many students and even teachers to regard philosophy as a "waste of time."

4. Problems with teaching methods:

It is noted that the existing format of classes does not allow the use of interactive methods of work, games, training, etc., which could take into account the interests and requests of students. The learning process becomes a script rather than a flexible process of adaptation to students.

5. Formalization of the educational process:

The learning process is perceived as the implementation of a pre-written script, which can lead to limited creativity of teachers and failure to take into account the specifics of students and their future professions. This is especially noticeable in the context of teaching philosophy, where dialogue and discussion are important.

6. Inadmissibility of deviation from what is written:

Teachers are faced with the inadmissibility of deviating from written scripts and texts, which can limit the creative approach to teaching philosophy.

One can criticize not only the formal aspects of teaching, but also the reluctance to take into account the individual characteristics of students, their interests and requests. In general, he puts forward a proposal for the need to revise the methods of teaching philosophy in universities and a more flexible approach to the educational process.

Philosophy of education in relation to the teaching profession

Philosophy of education in the context of teaching philosophy in universities should strive not only for the transfer of knowledge, but also for the formation of the student's personality and the conscious formation of a worldview. The task of the philosophy teacher turns into a deeper and more creative process aimed at influencing the student in the sphere of his "ultimate existence," including questions of life, death, their meaning and other fundamental aspects of human essence.

The infectiousness of philosophy

The professor notes that philosophy cannot simply be taught as an ordinary humanities discipline, but it can be "infected" if a student shows interest. This involves an informal and inspiring approach to teaching that encourages philosophy to enter students' thinking.

Relevance of problems of existence in the modern context

The relevance of philosophical questions about existence at the present time is discussed, especially in light of the double transition (civilizational and regional), a time of uncertainty of reality and a deep crisis of culture.

In the modern educational paradigm, moving away from the traditional bias in cognition, it becomes important to understand the dual context of human thinking: intersubjective and activity-based (constructive), as well as taking into account the dual nature of thinking as collective and individual processes.

Education is undergoing changes, shifting the emphasis from the transfer of knowledge to the organization and support of collective and individual activities of students. The teacher becomes an accompaniment, stimulating, organizing conditions for the activity and creativity of students. Internet, distance learning, webinars - new means of active educational activities.

In the conditions of developing technogenic civilization, education must adapt. This includes a new understanding of knowledge, taking into account the contexts of its use, as well as the formation of a methodological layer in science and education. The Internet plays a key role in reflecting new forms of life and reality. Subjects give way to learning tools, languages and forms, allowing students to design their own ways of learning and interacting with reality.

In this context, each content of education, especially in higher education, becomes unique and requires an individual construction methodology. Students are given the opportunity to independently create and construct both virtual and real worlds.

Teachers have a mission not only in teaching a specialty, but also in socialization. This includes compliance with functional requirements and the desire for a certain anthropological ideal in the conditions of modern sociality. However, the modern style of administration and the decline in cultural training of specialists jeopardize philosophical education. It is challenged by scientific and methodological meetings, and philosophy in technical universities is questioned. Disputes about fundamental and applied sciences, focused on a narrow industry, entail limiting the capabilities of specialists. Criteria for evaluating the work of philosophical groups, based on the number of publications, often do not contribute to the development of high-quality ideas.

Philosophical education at universities has become difficult in the context of the commercialization of science. Philosophy departments are faced with demands for income from publications, new courses and sponsorships, which causes disunity in university groups. The problems also affect technical specialties, where philosophy courses and preparation for entrepreneurship seem untenable. The solution to the crisis in philosophical education may be associated with a revival of interest in the practical aspects of the topics under discussion. The importance of philosophy in education is emphasized by its ability to provide a general picture of the world and philosophical justification for interdisciplinary approaches in science. Philosophy can also help bridge the gaps in meaning caused by major discoveries in science and is important for understanding the challenges of the 21st century. However, there is resistance to the inclusion of philosophy courses in the curriculum, perhaps due to a loss of interest in the subject within the university community.

Philosophy becomes inaccessible in the bustle of a consumer society, where pragmatism prevails over deep self-knowledge. The introduction of a master's degree creates a new educational form where students, focusing on a dissertation topic, can react negatively to tests and exams in philosophy. Overcoming the pragmatism of masters requires an approach that takes into account their professional specifics and research interests. Teachers must enter the sphere of interests of the audience, understand their "life world", and also adapt educational materials. It is important to attract the attention of a variety of master's streams, such as engineers, ecologists, economists, to philosophical issues, taking into account their different relationships to the history of science and philosophical problems. Reducing the hours of humanities subjects in educational programs requires the activity of teachers and the introduction of new educational technologies.

The study of methodological problems of modern science in a lecture course requires a detailed analysis of educational literature and orientation to the specialty. Literary analysis indicates a variety of approaches to the study of science from sociological, economic, political, legal, psychological, ethical, historical and philosophical positions. The lack of a unified knowledge about science outside the boundaries of his discipline makes a scientist an ordinary amateur in other fields. History and philosophy of science are useful for understanding the diversity of scientific disciplines and their current problems. Master's students who are focused on continuing their studies in graduate school must understand the significance of scientific and technical achievements, master the methods of argumentation, the rules of scientific work and the ethics of the scientific community. In the context of the transition to two-level education, an innovative approach to the content of training is required, including modernization of methods, technologization of educational activities and the use of a competency-based approach.

In conclusion, an analysis of the methodological problems of modern science in the context of philosophical education emphasizes not only the importance of studying this area, but also the lack of information resources covering modern methodological discussions. Despite the shortcomings, university teachers, including Moscow scientists, are actively introducing innovations into the educational process, providing students with knowledge about the interaction of science with social reality and key problems of the scientific community.

Analysis of the literature emphasizes the versatility of approaches to the study of science, presenting it from sociology, economics, psychology and other disciplines. The lack of uniform knowledge about science outside of a narrow specialization makes it urgent to introduce the history and philosophy of science into the educational process. These disciplines are able to provide students with a broad understanding of the diversity of scientific fields, their history and contemporary problems.

In the context of the transition to a two-level education system, especially in master's programs, it is important to adapt teaching methods to the specifics of master's training. The introduction of innovative methods, active learning and a competency-based approach contributes to more effective training of students oriented towards research activities.

Finally, in the context of current challenges and anti-scientism in popular culture, philosophical education plays a key role in developing an understanding of the value of scientific and technological achievements for society. Mastering the methodology of scientific research, the ability to give reasons for one's research approaches and comply with ethical standards become an integral part of the professional training of masters.

Control questions:

1. Do you agree with the thesis: "Philosophy is a science and a worldview? Why?
2. Why is the purpose of philosophy so important?
3. List the ancient Greek philosophers.
4. How many systems is philosophy divided into?
5. What is special about "Renaissance Philosophy"?

Topic 2: Stages of development of philosophy

Key words: ancient philosophy, Milesian school, Eleatic school, medieval philosophy, philosophers.

Ancient philosophy.

The concept of "ancient philosophy" occupies a very important place in the course of philosophy. This is the fundamental principle, the beginning of the emergence of philosophy. It gave impetus to the formation of modern philosophy, to the emergence of people's views and worldviews on the world and themselves. Our civilization is a subsidiary of antiquity. Ancient philosophy is included in philosophy as a historical part, one of the stages of philosophy, which lasted approximately from the 7th century. BC (starting from the Milesian school) to the feudal era (Middle Ages) V centuries. AD

The first period of ancient philosophy, which is called the classical stage. It lasted from the 2nd half. V century Don. e. to the 4th century Don. e. This period is associated with the activities of outstanding Greek philosophers - Socrates, Plato. Even those who have heard very little about philosophy, including ancient philosophy, nevertheless, at least once in their lives heard such a name as Plato (427-347 BC). This is an outstanding thinker of antiquity.

1) Milesian school (VII-VI centuries BC):

- • Thales: Considered one of the first philosophers. His main idea is the proposal of the material basis of all things, in his case - water.
- • Anaximander: Proposed the concept of an infinite and indefinite beginning (archaea), called "apeiron".

2) Eleatic school (VI-V centuries BC):

- • Parmenides: He dealt with the issues of being and non-being, arguing that the change and diversity of the world is an illusion, and true being is one and motionless.
- • Heraclitus: Opposed the idea of the permanence of the world. His famous fragment "Everything flows" emphasizes the constant change of the world.

3) Athenian philosophy (V century BC):

• Socrates: Main emphasis on ethics and the method of dialogue. Socrates did not write his works; his thoughts were transmitted through Plato's dialogues.

• Plato: Formulated a theory of ideas, considering the world to be changeable and an incomplete reflection of the world of ideas.

• Aristotle: Creator of a system covering all scientific knowledge of that time. Introduced the concepts of substance and act.

4) Hedonism and Stoicism (III-II centuries BC):

• Epicurus: Developed the idea of pleasure as the highest value, but not in the plane of pleasure, but as peace of mind.

• Seneca (Stoic): Claimed that man's power over himself is the only path to freedom.

Ancient philosophy shaped the main directions of thinking and served as a starting point for later philosophical movements. Her ideas turned out to be key to the formation of the fundamental principles of the Western philosophical tradition.

Medieval philosophy

Medieval philosophy covers the period from the 5th century to the 15th century and is characterized by the fusion of Christian theology with the philosophical thinking of antiquity. An important element of this period was the preservation and rethinking of the heritage of ancient philosophy in new religious and cultural conditions.

1) Patristics (II-VII centuries):

• Augustine the Blessed: Formulated the theory of predestination and the Fall, considered one of the founders of Christian philosophy.

• Basil the Great, Gregory of Nyssa: Engaged in the development of Christian theology and the foundations of faith.

2) Scholasticism (V-XV centuries):

• Anselm of Canterbury: Proposed the Ontology argument to prove the existence of God.
• Peter Abelar: Tried to combine faith and reason, put forward the concept of universals.
3) Revival of Aristotelianism (XIII-XV centuries):

• Duns Scotus: Contributed to the development of Aristotelianism, defended free will.

• William Occam: Developed the principle of simplicity (Occam's razor), separated faith from philosophy.

The Middle Ages left behind not only philosophical works, but also figures who became the founders of universities. Scholasticism, despite its limitations, contributed to the preservation and transmission of knowledge and the development of mental culture in difficult periods of history.

Renaissance and Enlightenment

Renaissance (XIV-XVII centuries):
The main features: the revival of ancient culture and interest in humanism, the development of science, art and education, the central place of man in culture.
• Representatives:
• Niccolo Machiavelli: The author of “The Prince” expressed a realistic vision of politics.

• Erasmus of Rotterdam: Promoted humanism and education, criticized the church.

• Thomas More: Author of "Utopia", which presents the image of an ideal society.

Enlightenment (XVII-XVIII centuries)

Main features: confidence in reason, science and education as the main engines of progress, criticism of despotism and absolutism, emphasis on individual freedom and human rights.

Representatives:

• Giovanni Pico della Mirandola: "Man is the creator of his own destiny," humanist and philosopher of the Renaissance.

• Giordano Bruno: Space explorer, convicted for his ideas about a vast universe.

• John Locke: "An Essay Concerning Human Understanding", the theory of tabula consideration and natural rights of man.

• Voltaire: Defended freedom of speech and religious tolerance, opposed absolutism.

• Jean-Jacques Rousseau: "On the Social Contract," expressed ideas about justice and democracy.

The Renaissance and Enlightenment represent eras in which the renewal of knowledge, the centrality of reason and liberation from tradition became key issues. The Renaissance revived interest in ancient culture, and the Enlightenment emphasized the role of reason in the progress of society, anticipating the values important to modern civilization.

Philosophy of the New Age (XVII-XVIII centuries)

The philosophy of the New Age is characterized by radical changes in methods of knowledge and views on the world. The main features of this stage in the history of philosophy include rationalism, empiricism, affirmation of the role of science and a departure from traditional scholasticism.

□ Francis Bacon (1561–1626):

Key ideas:

He proposed a new method of cognition - induction.

He advocated an empirical approach and called for the collection of factual material to generalize the laws of nature.

He criticized the Aristotelian tradition and scholasticism.

□ René Descartes (1596–1650):

Key ideas:

The fundamental method is doubt as the beginning of the philosophical path ("Cogito, ergo sum" - "I think, therefore I exist").

Rationalism: asserted the primacy of reason over experience.

Developed a mathematical method in philosophy.

□ Baruch Spinoza (1632–1677):

Key ideas:

Philosophical theory of pantheism (everything is God).

Rationalism: nature and divinity are not separate for Spinoza.

He rejected the classical idea of man as free will and introduced the concept of necessity.

□ John Locke (1632–1704):

Key ideas:

The theory of tabula consideration ("a slab that, before the experiment begins, is either clean or covered only with figures").

Empiricism: knowledge is gained from experience; had a negative attitude towards innate ideas.

The concept of limited government, with the basic idea of human rights to life, liberty and property.

The philosophy of modern times formed the basis of the scientific method and principles of empirical and rational knowledge, exerting a huge influence on the development of science and philosophy in subsequent periods.

Non-classical philosophy (late XIX - early XX century)

The period of non-classical philosophy is characterized by the destruction of classical metaphysical foundations and the search for new approaches to understanding man, society and knowledge. Among the representatives of this stage are Friedrich Nietzsche, Sigmund Freud and other thinkers whose ideas have made a significant contribution to modern philosophical discussions.

□ Friedrich Nietzsche (1844–1900):

Key ideas:

Criticism of traditional moral and religious values.

The concept of "will to power" and "inactive superman".

The contrast between the Apollonian and Dionysian principles in art and life.

□ Sigmund Freud (1856–1939)

Key ideas:

Theory of the unconscious and the structure of the psyche (ego, superego, id).

Oedipus complex and sexual aspects of psychology.

The method of psychoanalysis as a tool for revealing subconscious motivations.

 Martin Heidegger (1889–1976)

Key ideas:

Ontology of being: understanding the essence of being and human existence.

Criticism of technical rationality and analysis of everyday life.

The concept of "oblivion of being" and the problem of authenticity.

 Jean-Paul Sartre (1905–1980)

Key ideas:

Existentialism: freedom, responsibility, choice.

The concept of "existence precedes essence."

Analysis of the concepts of "being in itself" and "being for oneself".

Non-classical philosophy means rethinking established paradigms, including the rejection of some principles of dogmatic thinking and deeper attention to individual human experience. New approaches to the analysis of personality, society and culture are emerging, which will become the basis for further movements in philosophy and the humanities.

Philosophy of the Renaissance.

The Renaissance lasted approximately from the middle of the 14th century. until the middle of the 17th century. It received this name because at that time there was a huge interest in ancient culture, including philosophy. Some people even thought that antiquity had arisen again, had been revived, and that they were living in an ancient society. But time is irreversible, and the past does not return. There was not a revival of ancient culture, but its assimilation and use by people of subsequent times in accordance with their interests.

During the Renaissance, man (anthros) becomes the center of philosophical research - the time of anthropocentria comes. A new system of values has emerged, where man and nature come first, and then religion and its problems. The aesthetic (which in Greek means pertaining to feeling) dominates the philosophy of the Renaissance. Thinkers are more interested in the creativity and beauty of the human personality, rather than religious dogma. The basis of the anthropocentrism of the Renaissance lies in the change in economic relations. The separation of agriculture and crafts, the rapid development of manufacturing, marked the transition from feudalism to early capitalism.

In the philosophy of the Renaissance, the following directions are distinguished:

• humanistic (14-18 centuries) - human problems were solved, his greatness and power were affirmed, the dogmas of the church were denied (Petrarch, L. Valli);

• Neoplatonic (15-16 centuries) - from the standpoint of idealism they tried to understand natural phenomena, space, human problems, developed the teachings of Plato (N. Kuzansky, Marandola, Paracelsus);

• natural philosophy (16th - 17th centuries) - based on scientific and astronomical discoveries, they made an attempt to change the idea of the structure of the Universe, the Cosmos and the foundations of the universe (Nicholas Copernicus, Giordano Bruno, G. Galileo);

• reformation (14-17 centuries) - an attempt to revise church ideology and the relationship between people and the church (Erasmus of Rotterdam, John Calvin, Marty Luther, Thomas Munzer, Usenlief);

• political (15th century) - associated with problems of government (Nicolo Machiavelli);

• utopian-socialist (15-17 centuries) - the search for an ideal society based on the regulation of all relationships by the state in the absence of private property (Thomas More, Tommaso Kempanella).

The Renaissance began in Italy earlier than in other Western European countries. The first representative of the Renaissance is considered to be the Italian poet and philosopher Francesco Petrarca (1304 – 1374). He is widely known for his sonnet poems dedicated to his beloved woman. Petrarch is the founder of Western European lyric poetry of subsequent times, in which the feelings, experiences, impressions, moods of the authors of poems, their inner spiritual world are expressed. Interest in man, his life and worldview is also characteristic of the philosophy of the Renaissance.

At that time there was a close connection between philosophy, fiction, art and science. The Renaissance is a time of intensive development of art, the creation of magnificent works of art. Outstanding representatives of

Renaissance culture: English poet and playwright William Shakespeare, Italian artist, scientist, inventor and philosopher Leonardo da Vinci, Italian sculptor, artist, architect and poet Michelangelo Buonarroti, scientists Nicolaus Copernicus (Poland), Galileo Galilei (Italy), Johann Kepler (Germany) and others.

In conclusion, consideration of the stages of development of philosophy from antiquity to the non-classical era allows us to see not only the evolution of philosophical ideas, but also their influence on the formation of the cultural, social and scientific context. Each stage carries its own unique features and characteristics, reflecting the spirit of the times and the challenges facing the thinkers of their era.

In antiquity, philosophy arose as an attempt to explain the nature and place of man in the world, leading to a keen interest in questions of being, knowledge and morality. The Middle Ages, in turn, meant the influence of religious tradition on philosophical reflection, where theology played a leading role. The Renaissance and Enlightenment highlighted the need for the scientific method, rational thinking and the desire for liberation from tradition.

Modern philosophy, beginning with philosophers such as Bacon and Descartes, focused on the role of man in the process of knowledge and the search for truth, noting the need for scientific method and mathematical clarity. German classical philosophy, represented by Kant and Hegel, continued these studies, delving into issues of knowledge and ethics.

During the period of non-classical philosophy, with Friedrich Nietzsche, Sigmund Freud and others, the focus shifts to the individual, the unconscious, freedom and the meaning of life. These thinkers questioned established norms and sought new ways to understand man and society.

Each era that contributed to philosophy provided the foundation for further research and the formation of modern philosophical movements. Philosophy, being a living dialogue with time, continues to inspire and provoke thinkers in their quest to understand the deep questions of existence, the meaning of life and the nature of human knowledge.

CONTROL QUESTIONS:

1. EXPLAIN THE CONCEPT OF "ANCIENT PHILOSOPHY".
2. BASIC CONCEPTS AND STAGES OF DEVELOPMENT OF PHILOSOPHY.
3. THE MAIN STAGES OF THE HISTORICAL DEVELOPMENT OF PHILOSOPHY.
4. WHAT IS THE PECULIARITY OF MEDIEVAL PHILOSOPHY?
5. DIRECTIONS OF PHILOSOPHY DURING THE RENAISSANCE.

Topic 3: Ontology, epistemology and philosophy of consciousness.

Key words: ontology, epistemology, philosophy of consciousness, epistemological optimism, epistemological pessimism, problem of consciousness.

Ontology

Ontology is a branch of philosophy that studies existence. In the classical sense, ontology is knowledge about the extremely general. The term "ontology" was first proposed by R. Gocklenius in 1613 in his "Philosophical Dictionary", and then by J. Clauberg in 1656 in the work "Metaphysika de ente, quae rectus Ontosophia". In practical use, the term was fixed by H. Wolf, who clearly separated the semantics of the terms “ontology” and “metaphysics”. The fundamental question of ontology is what exists. The basic concepts of ontology include: being, structure, properties, forms of being (material, ideal, existential), space, time, movement. Thus, ontology is an attempt at the most general description of the existing universe, which is not limited to the data of individual sciences and, perhaps, cannot be reduced to them.

American philosopher Willard Quine presents ontology as the content of a certain theory. It says that it includes the objects that the theory assumes to exist.

Questions of ontology have ancient roots in European philosophy. They go back to the Pre-Socratics and especially Parmenides. Plato and Aristotle made significant contributions to the development of ontological problems. The existence of abstract objects (universals) was central to medieval philosophy.

Twentieth-century philosophers such as Nicolaus Hartmann ("new ontology") and Martin Heidegger ("fundamental ontology") dealt specifically with ontological problems. In modern philosophy, ontological problems of consciousness are of particular interest.

The main object of ontology is existence; being, which is described as the completeness and unity of all types of reality: objective, physical, subjective, social and virtual. Reality is traditionally associated with matter (material world) and spirit (spiritual world, including the concepts of God and soul).

Being, as something conceivable, is opposed to the unthinkable nothingness. In phenomenology and existentialism, being is identified with man as the only one with the ability to think and question about being. However, in classical metaphysics, being means God.

Epistemology

Epistemology is one of the philosophical disciplines that studies the processes and methods of cognition. In turn, it differs from epistemology in that it explores the relationship between the subject of knowledge (the researcher) and the object of knowledge (the object being studied). According to the basic scheme of analysis of cognition, it includes a conscious subject and an object of nature, which is considered independent of the subject's consciousness.

Epistemology touches on many problems, including the interpretation of the subject and object of cognition, various structural aspects of the cognitive process, as well as questions about truth and its criteria, forms and methods of cognition.

In ancient Greek philosophy, knowledge was considered a single whole, where the object and knowledge about it were not separated. However, with the development of medieval scholasticism, epistemology became more diversified, and ideas about dual truth and multiple paradigms led to the emergence of new models of the cognitive process. Movements such as realism, nominalism and conceptualism also contributed to the development of epistemology.

The emergence of natural sciences raised the question of how to achieve true knowledge. This led to the opposition between sensationalism and rationalism, and then to empiricism and rationalism in the 17th and 18th centuries. The problem of the subject's activity in the process of cognition became important thanks to the works of Berkeley and Hume. Kant played a key role in overcoming the attitudes of naturalistic epistemology and criticizing metaphysical philosophical constructions, focusing on identifying the subjective foundations of knowledge.

Philosophers of the transcendental-critical school presented the problem of multiple foundations of knowledge and the relativity of truth, distinguishing between the content and form of thinking. Their rejection of metaphysics and the development of the natural sciences brought knowledge of the world to the center of philosophy. This epistemological problematic became important for neo-Kantianism and positivism.

Classical epistemology connected the foundations of knowledge with an isolated subject, which led to limited knowledge and psychologism. Philosophers tried to overcome these limitations, but were aware of the fundamental limitations of the original epistemological abstractions and assumptions.

Methodological reflection on the development of the humanities was of particular importance in criticizing the foundations of classical philosophy and rejecting abstractions about a self-conscious and isolated subject. Contemporary research documents the limitations of subject-object schemas and introduces new structural divisions and abstractions, including practice, paradigm, and language. Traditional epistemological problems are included in a broader sociocultural context and system of concepts. Methodology of science and epistemology occupy a central place within the framework of epistemology.

Philosophy of consciousness

Consciousness is the highest form of human mental activity. It combines thinking, feeling, emotional and volitional processes. Consciousness not only allows you to perceive the world, but also change it in accordance with subjective life goals.

This aspect distinguishes man from all other living beings. This is obvious to most people at the common sense level. The definition of consciousness is complex and of fundamental importance to the humanities and social sciences. Various fields of knowledge, such as anthropology, psychology, law and cybernetics, use the concept of consciousness in their theoretical constructs and practice, including psychiatry. However, they often accept ready-made definitions and criteria of consciousness, leaving the study of its essence to philosophy.

There is a deep connection between the mystery of man's consciousness and his being. Consciousness and man are inextricably linked with each other and are identical. According to the theory of evolution, the mental organization of our ape-like ancestors gradually became more complex and led to the emergence of consciousness.

However, the hypothesis about the origin of man from monkeys no longer corresponds to new discoveries in science. Genetic studies of Neanderthals have shown that they are not our direct ancestors. The question of the origin of the first man still remains unanswered, so there is no final explanation of the origin of consciousness.

However, several facts have been established regarding consciousness:

• Consciousness is not limited to simply acquiring knowledge about the external world for adaptation;

• Consciousness directly depends on the complex functioning of the human brain;

• The development and functioning of consciousness influences the social and cultural environment;

• Consciousness is historical and subject to change over time;

• Consciousness has both individual and supra-individual aspects.

Many children are forced to grow up around animals for various reasons. An example of such a child is Mowgli from R. Kipling's fairy tale. These children do not have consciousness, although their brains are developed. When people find them, they are almost indistinguishable from the animals they grew up among. The process of their transformation into people is long and difficult.

A person has consciousness from birth, but it is implicit. Just like a seed already contains a tree and its fruits. For a tree to grow, it needs soil, moisture, warmth, light, pollination, and protection. To develop consciousness, a person needs active interaction with others, overcoming resistance and pressure. The revelation of consciousness occurs through human efforts.

Language plays an important role in the socialization of a person and his inclusion in culture. It is a system of signs through which people express their thoughts, communicate and transmit information. There are natural and artificial languages: the first include speech, facial expressions, gestures and body movements, the second - the language of mathematics, painting, road signs, etc.

The connection between language and consciousness is close. Language is involved in the perception of the world, serves as the basis for memory and allows us to recognize emotions. Even the inner speech we make in our thoughts about ourselves is based on language.

Language allows us to study and objectify consciousness, making it accessible to other people. The history of language is the history of consciousness. The vocabulary reflects the thoughts of the people, and the syntax reflects their way of thinking. Plasticity and internal dissection are features of language.

Labor is the activity of people aimed at changing the world around them in order to improve living conditions. Unlike animals, humans have diverse needs that cannot be satisfied by nature alone. The main way to satisfy these needs is work, in which a person actively interacts with nature, determining its course. Nature is seen as a passive object on which man influences.

Thanks to work, the basic functions of the hands develop, speech is formed, the senses are strengthened and the psyche develops. Purposeful activity begins with the manufacture of tools, with the help of which the impact on nature is carried out. Tools must be suitable for both humans and the natural object in order to achieve the desired results.

Control questions:

1. What is epistemology?

2. What is the difference between epistemological pessimism and optimism?

3. Forms of consciousness.

4. What is the main thing in consciousness?

Topic 4: Methods, laws and categories of philosophy.

Key words: methods of philosophy, metaphysics, dialectics, laws of philosophy, categories of philosophy.

Methods of philosophy

The methodology of knowledge describes the methods and methods used in various sciences to obtain knowledge. It represents a general scientific approach that helps to understand the relationships and causes of change in all phenomena.

In the history of philosophy, various methods of knowledge have been developed, such as metaphysics, sophistry, eclecticism, dialectics, synergetics. The sophists tried to replace true knowledge with false knowledge by exploiting various flaws in natural language, such as amonymy, amphaboly, and incorrect word connections. Farabi called sophistry "false wisdom."

Metaphysics, on the contrary, operates mainly with objects, denying the sophistic method. Unlike sophistic thinking, metaphysical thinking takes into account the material basis of the phenomenon under discussion.

Metaphysical thinking strives to study objects very carefully and reveal their essence very deeply. However, its main drawback is that it does not see and does not want to see the connections between objects and natural phenomena, their constant change and development.

Eclecticism, on the contrary, unites different, even opposing sides without clear principles, without paying attention to the difference between the important and the unimportant, the main and the secondary. Its main drawback is that it is not able to distinguish the main, decisive connection in the relations between objects and phenomena of the real world.

In its inception, dialectics was a method of understanding truth through discussion and debate. Later it came to be used to understand and explain the world. The dialectical approach to thinking differs from the sophistic and metaphysical in that it views objects and their images as closely related and free from the shortcomings of sophistry and metaphysics. In dialectical thinking, objects and their logical images or concepts are considered as natural elements of cognition.

The dialectical approach requires taking into account all aspects and connections of objects or phenomena of the world, as well as their relationships with other objects and phenomena. He considers objects and phenomena not only in connection, but also in movement, change and development.

One important feature of the dialectical method is the concrete historical approach to the study of objects and phenomena. To fully understand the essence of an object, it is important to consider it in the context of its external environment, conditions, location and time. Neglecting this approach can lead to one-sidedness in theory and practice.

The dialectical method reveals the essence of objects, their relationships and patterns of development with the help of philosophical laws and concepts. The laws and concepts of dialectics reflect the general connections of objects and phenomena in reality, which allows us to understand the laws of their development and consciously analyze events occurring in practice.

In the 20th century, the concept of “synergetics” appeared in science - a method for studying the laws of self-organization of disordered states in reality. It is applicable in the study of disordered, unstable, nonequilibrium, nonlinear relationships in open systems. Thus, the correct use of the synergetic method contributes to understanding the patterns of self-organization in reality.

There are several methods for obtaining knowledge scientifically. One such method is observation. It allows you to study objects with a specific purpose, and its level depends on the specific purpose and knowledge about the object. Observation can be direct (without instruments) and indirect (using instruments), expanding the possibilities of perception.

Measuring objects helps determine their quantitative characteristics by comparison with objects that have precisely fixed properties. It helps establish properties such as strength and complexity. Comparison is the stage at which the similarities and differences of an object are established, based on previous knowledge.

Experiment is another research method that allows you to study objects through tests and experiments. This method helps to gain deep knowledge about the qualities of an object and its relationships with other phenomena. Depending on the field of study, the experiment can be either physical or mental.

At the theoretical level, there are several methods of scientific knowledge.

The first of them is the axiomatic method, based on axioms that are accepted as valid in a specific theoretical system without proof. Theoretical knowledge is derived deductively from these axioms.

The second method is hypothetico-deductive, using experimental data as a basis. Hypotheses can be confirmed or refuted in experiments, which guides scientific research and contributes to the search for new evidence and information.

The third method is the method of ascent from the abstract to the concrete, which allows us to present the phenomenon being studied as a set of various connections. The main goal of this method is to highlight connections and reflect them using scientific abstractions.

Induction and deduction play an important role in cognition. Induction helps to generalize the knowledge of individual cases, discovering patterns and establishing cause-and-effect relationships between objects. Deduction, on the contrary, is used to study evidence and is used in the theories of science.

Analogy allows us to study similar features of objects, and idealization creates abstract idealized objects for a better understanding of reality. Modeling, being a scientific method, is based on the analogy between an object and its model, helping to study complex objects.

The method of systematization is widely used to study complex objects, allowing one to study their interconnected elements as a single system. Hypotheses, ideas, facts, laws and theories also play an important role in scientific knowledge, helping to deepen the understanding of objects.

Laws of philosophy

Knowledge of the laws of the objective world allows humanity to understand its secrets. Philosophical laws help to comprehend changes in the world, processes of emergence and disappearance, as well as the interaction and development of objects and phenomena of the objective world. The category “law” reflects important, necessary, internal, recurring, general and relatively stable connections and relationships between objects and phenomena of the objective world, determining the features and direction of development of events in specific conditions.

It is necessary to distinguish between the laws of existence and legal laws; the former are objective in nature and can be used in practice, in contrast to the latter, which are developed by people to maintain order in society. It is important to note the difference between the concepts of “law” and “regularity”: a law specifically reflects the aspects of a pattern, while a pattern is a general trend that manifests itself as a cycle of laws. The laws of material reality are diverse and depend on objective processes in nature and society.

The laws of nature exist long before man appeared on earth, while the laws of society arose due to human activity. The laws of society reflect the most important dependencies in social relations. Another difference is that natural laws change gradually, while social laws operate over a period of time and can be replaced by new ones. According to the scope of action, laws are divided into universal, general and particular; examples of general laws are the laws of conservation of energy and universal gravitation.

Universal laws make it possible to understand changes and developments in nature, society and thinking.

Philosophical laws, which will be discussed further, are part of these universal laws.

The philosophy is based on the idea of the relationship between quantitative and qualitative changes. This law states that even small quantitative changes over time can lead to radical qualitative changes.

In the real world, all objects and phenomena have unique qualities that distinguish them from each other. Quality is determined by the totality of properties and features of each object.

Quality is a unifying element and ensures the integrity and relative stability of the object. A change in quality necessarily entails a change in properties, but a change in properties does not always lead to a change in quality.

Each object is unique and interconnected with others in the system. An example is a table that has both natural qualities (made of wood) and social ones (as a product of human labor).

Objects also differ in quantitative characteristics, such as volume, size, speed and temperature. In society and in nature, quantitative and qualitative aspects can be distinguished, differing in development, labor productivity, culture, etc.

The basis of objects is laid in their quantitative and qualitative characteristics, which always influence each other. No object has only quantitative or only qualitative properties - they are always present together. It is their combination that allows a complete description of the subject.

The concept of "measure" reflects the connection between quantity and quality - this is the correspondence of the quantitative characteristics of an object to its quality. The quantity of an item varies within its quality. New quantitative characteristics show the measure of the relationship between quantity and quality, which determines the specificity of the object.

There are ordinary measures, systemic substantial measures and precise measures, which also exist in public life. The concepts of quality, quantity and measure are objective and general characteristics of the world, therefore the statement about the subjectivity of the quality of objects is unjustified.

Quality and quantity are interrelated and relative. Their boundaries are changeable and cannot be absolute. It is important to understand the exact state of these changes in science and practice, as the world is constantly moving and evolving.

Quantitative changes lead to new qualitative characteristics, and new qualitative properties exhibit new quantitative characteristics. For example, a new breed of sheep may produce more and longer wool than previous ones.

Changes in theoretical and practical activities include quantitative and qualitative aspects and are a complex process. Revolutionary and evolutionary changes are separated, and the transition between qualitative states occurs in the form of a leap. This leap is a philosophical concept meaning a transition from quantitative to qualitative changes, which occurs much faster than continuous change. Leaps usually arise as a result of the accumulation of quantitative changes, representing the resolution of contradictions and the emergence of new qualities. Thus, the leap denies the old quality and establishes a new one.

Qualitative changes occur in various spheres of society, such as social, economic, political, cultural and moral, raising society and the state to new levels of development. They do not arise spontaneously, but are the result of the creative and social activity of broad sections of the population.

In the world, all things and events have their opposites, which influence each other, leading to the emergence of the new and the disappearance of the old. This process reflects the law of unity and interaction of opposites. It is important to note that all things are different and no two things are exactly alike. The differences may be important or minor.

Contradictions and opposites underlie the differences between things and events. Dialectical contradiction is the interaction of opposite sides and tendencies inherent in things and events, which stimulates their development and movement. This is manifested in the fact that different aspects of things and events exclude each other, but at the same time presuppose.

Relations between opposite sides of things and events are defined as contradictions. Collision, as opposed to contradiction, means the strengthening of opposing sides of things and events to such an extent that they cannot exist within the same framework. For example, an atom is made up of negative and positive charges, protons and electrons, which is a complex example of opposites.

The development of the organic world is also impossible without the interaction of opposites. Life itself is a contradictory process, including contradictory aspects such as creation and decay, assimilation and dissimilation.

The law of unity and interaction of opposites also manifests itself in the process of cognition. Cognition consists of interconnected rational and sensory cognition. Sensory cognition is limited to the external aspects of things and events, while abstract thinking reveals their internal connections.

Contradictions are inherent in all things and events of the world, from their appearance to their disappearance. The unity of opposites expresses different aspects of one essence. Therefore, contradictions exist within one thing and are interconnected. They can also transform into and penetrate each other, giving rise to new forms of matter.

The interaction of opposites is both absolute and temporary. Specific forms of interaction may change, but the phenomenon itself remains unchanged. Natural and social contradictions are varied and can be resolved in various ways, such as replacing the old with the new or merging contradictions to move forward.

The process of development involves the rejection of the old in favor of the new, while maintaining the positive aspects of the past. The dialectical approach recognizes the creative role of negation and emphasizes its importance for development. Internal contradictions lead to the decomposition of the old and the emergence of the new.

Differences between objects and phenomena act as the basis for contradictions and opposites, which are mutually intertwined and serve as a source of development and movement. The negation of the old in favor of the new reflects the progress and development of the material world, based on the principle of continuity and consistency.

The law of negation is applicable to various phenomena and processes in the real world and in knowledge. For example, when a grain is placed in soil, it germinates under the influence of heat and moisture, turning into a plant. It denies itself as a grain, and the new plant denies itself as a grain, and so on. This law also manifests itself in the moral life of society. Hegel described it by talking about the division of the original whole thought into contradictory elements, which are expressed through "yes" and "no", and lead to the emergence of antithesis.

Dialectical negation means development and manifests itself in changes in the states of objects under the influence of external factors. For example, when heated, water turns into steam, and when cooled, it becomes water again. This is the negation of one state by another, but is not development, but rather a change of state. Dialectical negation, on the contrary, resolves such contradictions and leads to a higher level of development.

Denial of negation completes a certain stage of development, while simultaneously serving as a starting point for further development. It also means time as the final stage of a certain process, which is the starting point for a new dialectical sequence.

A philosophical category is a general concept that reflects the important properties and relationships of objects and phenomena in the real world. They represent a form of thinking that reflects the general laws of the development of the world in human consciousness.

Categories differ from the concepts of other sciences in several fundamental features. Firstly, they reflect the most general connections in the objective world and are a form of human thinking. Secondly, categories have logical content that allows you to understand the essence of objects and phenomena. Thirdly, categories play a methodological role in scientific knowledge, helping to understand and study the patterns of development of objects and phenomena of the world.

Category	Ancient philosophy	Medieval philosophy	Philosophy of the New Age
Substance, the root cause of existence	Thales: the origin of all things is water ("arche"); The earth is a flat disk that rests on water. Anaximander: the first principle "apeiron" is the eternal, immeasurable, infinite substance from which everything	Creationism: The ultimate cause of all things is God. Space, nature, phenomena of the surrounding world are the creation of God. God created the world around us out of nothing. The creation of the world is the result of an act	Hegel: substance - Absolute idea, pure rational thinking. It exists forever and contains in a hidden "folded" form all possible definitions of natural, social and spiritual phenomena.

	arose, everything consists and into which everything will turn. Anaximenes: the root cause of everything is air. All substances on Earth are the result of different concentrations of air. Heraclitus: the beginning is fire. Pythagoras: the root cause of everything is number. Unit is the smallest particle of everything	of Divine will	Schopenhauer: the first cause of the world is the metaphysical first will as an insatiable, strong attraction, a dark, dull impulse. Will is a self-sufficient principle, something akin to the inscrutable forces of the universe
Being	Parmenides: divided the sensory and	Augustine: true being is God. The	Hegel: being is the absolute and

	speculative world, while the sensory (material) is the fruit of deceptive delusions, and being is something that can be thought about and talked about, i.e. speculative world. Being is eternal, motionless, indivisible. Zeno: separated sensory knowledge and the highest spiritual ideal. Everything that exists is a material expression of ideas. Sophists: being is	physical world is only involved in existence, because created by God, therefore it is finite. W. Occam's nominalism: only concrete things themselves really exist, while general concepts (universals) are only names of things. Universals exist not before, but after things, they exist in the human mind, and things are known through sensory experience.	the universe, i.e. Absolute idea. The absolute idea is reason, therefore, the essence of its existence is self-knowledge. Existence is changeable - it is a process of constant interaction between being and nothingness, as a result of which something appears. Existentialism: it is necessary to distinguish between existence and being. Existence is everything that exists. Being is determined by the

	subjective, i.e. The criterion of being is not its immobility, but its infinity. Each person lives in the world of his own sensations.		individual, therefore, being is formed through the formation of a person's experiences of himself in the world around him
Movement	Heraclitus: the source of any movement is the inconsistency of internal processes. He characterized fire as "all flaming and all dying out," as the substance of all changes. The material fundamental principle is constantly identical to	Eschatologism: history is determined by divine providence, it has a direction, a vector of movement. The movement is expressed by its flow from the "earthly city" to the "city of God" or from the earthly pagan kingdoms to the kingdom of Christ.	Deism: God created the world and did not interfere with the affairs of this world anymore. The universe continued to exist independently, obeying natural laws. Movement as change is a consequence of the laws of nature. Pantheism: a philosophical

	itself and at the same time is in a state of constant change. Democritus and Leucippus: motion is an attribute of matter. Everything that exists is made of atoms and emptiness. Emptiness is as real as atoms and is a necessary condition for their movement	Providentialism: the concept of the universal animation of matter, as well as the activity of matter through endowing it with life	doctrine that asserts the identity of nature and God. Movement is a transition from one mode of God to another, while movement as a change is rational (Spinoza)

Space and time		Августин: время - это человеческий способ обозначения изменения и поэтому в объективном смысле не существует. Время есть мера движения и изменения. Ни прошедшее, ни будущее не имеют реального существования. Оно присуще только настоящему	Э. Беркли, Д. Юм: пространство и время - это собственные чувственные впечатления человека. Человек не знает ничего кроме данных своего сознания, поэтому познаются не объективные вещи, а их субъективные образы.

So, philosophical categories play an important role in cognition, allowing people to gain new knowledge about the world and predict its future development. Philosophical categories are formed based on how people interact with the material world and perceive it through the senses. They reflect the relationship between a person and the world around him and are a product of social practice. In this process, logical categories are formed that reflect the patterns of the external world.

The categories of other sciences indicate specific areas of connections in nature, society and thinking, while philosophical categories reflect the most general relationships in the objective world. Philosophical categories can be divided into three groups according to their nature and functions.

The first group includes categories that reflect the most general connections of reality, such as individual, particular, general, essence and phenomenon. The second group denotes the structure of reality, including the categories of content and form, whole and part, structure and element. The third group of categories indicates determinism between objects and phenomena of reality, including cause and effect, necessity and chance, possibility and reality.

The philosophical categories "individual" and "general" reflect the dialectical unity and difference between objects and phenomena of reality. "Singular" reflects what is inherent in only one object or phenomenon, while "general" reflects the identity between objects within a specific qualitative definition. "Special" is an intermediate category between "single" and "general". Philosophical categories play an important role in the process of cognition, being strongholds from ignorance to knowledge.

Objects and phenomena of reality are described using various categories, such as content and form, whole and part, structure and element. Content includes internal elements and their relationships that describe a specific object or phenomenon, while form determines the way the content is expressed. For example, the content of an atom is its elementary particles and their movement, and the form is the order of arrangement of these elementary particles and their structure.

Content and form are inseparable from each other in every object and phenomenon. First the content changes, and then the form. However, form actively influences the development of content. The unity of content and form does not exclude the opposition between them. Development is possible only if content and form correspond to each other. Therefore, resolving contradictions between content and form plays an important role in scientific knowledge and practice.

Element and structure form a unity of opposites. Elements change and interact while the structure strives for stability. This contradiction is resolved at a certain stage of development, when the old structure does not correspond to the changed elements, and the process of destruction of the old and the formation of a new structure occurs.

Wholeness and part are philosophical concepts. Any object consisting of interconnected parts is a whole, expressing the unity of diversity. The variety of parts, their differences and quality are characteristics of the whole. The principle of causality reflects the interconnection of events in the objective world, meaning that the cause influences the result. A cause is the influence of an object or event that causes changes in another object or event under certain conditions.

Control questions:

1. Basic methods of philosophy.
2. How are objects considered in metaphysics?
3. The difference between eclecticism and dogmatism.

4. List the laws of philosophy.

5. Movement in ancient philosophy.

Topic 5: Philosophy of society. Global problems of modern society and prospects for the development of society.

Key words: philosophy of society, global problems of modern society, prospects for the development of society.

The social structure of society comes from nature, which attracted the attention of philosophers to the importance of natural laws in the formation of social relations. Various concepts examine social connections from the perspective of biological laws, anthropological principle, or social contract theory.

Sociology analyzes relationships between people based on an understanding of their actions, intentions and goals. Structural-functional analysis focuses on the study of the relationship between the structure and function of classes necessary for the stable functioning of society as a system.

In the past, the activity approach to understanding social interactions prevailed, but today attention is shifting to individual aspects of life rather than to mass social groups. The emergence of community between people presupposes similarity, openness, mutual influence and interaction of inner life.

Social philosophy sets itself the task of understanding the conditions of unification, integrity and meaning of society, which distinguishes it from other social sciences. Modern social philosophy also seeks to find out under what conditions the most effective interaction between the individual and society can be achieved.

The problem of the laws of functioning and development of society is extremely important, and social philosophy is recognized as a scientific field of knowledge. In modern conditions, civil society is of particular importance, which aims to ensure individual rights and freedoms on the basis of equality before the law.

In his work "The Open Society and Its Enemies," Karl Popper used the term "open society," taken from A. Bergson's book "The Two Sources of Morality and Religion" (1932). He paid great attention to the study of "open" and "closed" societies, considering this one of his most important studies.

According to the concept of A. Bergson, a "closed society" is a society where people are subject to social and moral norms, transmitted through customs and traditions in the form of strict regulations or taboos. Here, morality and religion play the role of a system of primary biological impulses of the body.

The closed nature of society leads to the formation of fear and hostility towards other societies, cultures, and religions. However, at certain stages of the development of society, this contributes to the unity of people and the success of their collective efforts, which can be maintained under certain circumstances.

Openness of society implies active interaction of political, ideological and religious views, economic freedom, the absence of psychological and legal barriers to property and entrepreneurship, as well as the availability of cultures and information under reasonable restrictions. An important characteristic of an "open society" is the openness of people to each other and personal freedom, which is possible only in a free society.

Social philosophy not only explores and explains its specialized aspects, but also develops effective methods of knowledge.

Modern philosophy views society as an integral system consisting of interconnected parts and elements that constantly interact with each other. This idea has its roots in ancient Greek thought, where society was viewed as an orderly whole made up of individual parts. Such views arose from the dialectical way of thinking found in Ancient Greece. In the context of the systematic nature of social life, philosophers and sociologists of the 19th and 20th centuries studied the structure and changes of society. Modern social philosophy identifies four main characteristics of society: self-activity, self-organization, self-development and self-sufficiency. Individual subsystems cannot be self-sufficient; only all taken together create a self-sufficient system. The balance between change and stability is an important aspect for the continuation of a complex system such as a society even though it is constantly changing.

Society consists of the main types of social activities that constantly function within its structure. These types include material activities, spiritual activities, managerial activities and service activities, also known as humanitarian or social activities.

The traditional approach of philosophical thought identifies the following spheres of society: material-economic, social, political and spiritual. Both approaches have a right to exist, as they complement each other to some extent. However, the modern level of development of socio-philosophical thought more justifies the first approach.

All human activity consists of four elements: people, physical things, symbols and the connections between them. Activity is a specific human form of active relationship to the world around us, including purposeful understanding, change and transformation of the world.

Man is a key element in any activity. Activity can be directed at other people, at things, or at symbols and signs. For the formation of social action, connections between these elements are necessary. The main types of social activity correspond to these elements; each sphere of social activity has its own specifics and plays a role in the life of society.

Global problems of modern society and prospects for the development of society

Over the course of human history, outdated technologies and social methods of interaction with nature have been abandoned. Initially, people were subordinate to nature and adapted to its changes, changing their own essence. As production forces developed, an instrumental attitude toward nature and toward oneself began to prevail. As a result, by the beginning of the third millennium, humanity was faced with a crisis of its civilization, which affected environmental, social, demographic, economic and other aspects.

The current global situation indicates a crisis in human consumer attitudes towards natural and social resources. This crisis arose as a result of the development of modern civilization and became a pressing problem of industrial society. It is important to understand the causes and relationships of global problems in human development and find ways to solve them.

The existence of global problems is widely recognized, but the question of how to solve them and the prospects for human development remains a matter of debate. The concept of "global problem" does not have a clear definition.

In the scientific community, there are three main approaches to understanding global problems. Some proponents of the first approach believe that all social problems can eventually become global. Others support the idea that only the most dangerous problems that require immediate intervention are global, such as preventing wars and solving environmental problems. The third approach is based on a comprehensive analysis of the characteristics of a global problem, highlighting such criteria as universal character, planetary scale and the need for the united efforts of all humanity to solve them.

There are different approaches to classifying global problems at present. One of the largest and most developed approaches is based on correlating a global problem with the level of a global catastrophe, in accordance with the classification of disasters proposed by A. Azimov.

In this case, the source and level of threat to the existence of human civilization is used as a classification criterion. According to A. Azimov's classification of threats, all possible disasters are divided into 5 classes.

Class 1 disasters include those associated with changes in the properties of the Universe observed during the processes of its expansion and contraction. Class 2 catastrophes are caused by processes occurring on the Sun and its evolution.

Class 3 disasters are associated with changes in planet Earth. Such disasters include, for example, bombardment of the Earth by space objects, slowdown of the planet's rotation, changes in weather and magnetic field, mutations under the influence of cosmic rays.

The death of humanity while maintaining other components of the Earth's biosphere constitutes the essence of class 4 disasters. These include, in particular, species competition, infectious diseases, mutations under the influence of anthropogenic factors. Class 5 disasters are caused by the degradation of human society and the self-destruction of civilization.

Level 5 disasters are now becoming a real threat to the existence of humanity, while level 1-4 disasters are more theoretical in nature. Problems, the presence of which can lead to catastrophes of this level, are essentially global problems of our time. These problems can be divided into 3 main groups.

There are 3 options for the future development of humanity. They depend on the willingness and ability to solve problems. The first option involves continued environmental destruction and economic dominance. It also includes national egoism, rigidity of consciousness and the inability to adequately respond to threats.

The second option is the establishment of a world dictatorship in relation to the countries of the "third world" and its own population. The third option involves awareness of the threats of the environmental crisis, a new worldview and values based on global collective action.

Development according to the first two scenarios can lead to disaster: degradation, depletion of natural resources or global military conflict.

The third scenario is the most acceptable, but also the most complicated. Development options range from pessimistic to optimistic. The prospects for human development depend on how early this process begins. The later development begins, the more effort and time the world community will need to solve global problems.

Restoration and preservation of natural ecosystems to the required extent is a necessary condition, but not sufficient. In light of the search for extraterrestrial civilizations, many years of research indicate the possible danger of self-destruction of civilizations, which is supported by the absence of signs of intelligence in the Universe.

It appears that natural threats are associated with moral development that is not in keeping with the scientific progress of civilization. An example is the events of September 11, 2001, when airplanes became an instrument of horror. Therefore, moral development is important to prevent disasters. Immoral actions can lead to global disasters.

The solution to the problem is to be guided by moral criteria. But this is ignored in real life. The gap between the moral level and scientific and technological progress is the main problem. Without solving it, it is impossible to solve other global problems.

The global crisis in attitudes towards natural and social resources reflects the situation in which humanity finds itself. There is a need for harmonization of connections in the global system and human spiritual development. The solution to this complex problem will determine the prospects for the development of human civilization.

Control questions:

1. The main functions of social philosophy.

2. When did the concept of “global problems” appear?

3. What problems are considered global?

4. What human qualities are important for the survival of civilization in the modern era?

Topic 6: The importance of logical thinking in teaching practice.

Key words: human thinking, logic, the meaning of logical thinking, development of logical thinking, deduction, induction.

Logical thinking plays a central role in the modern education system for several important reasons:

1. Teaching critical thinking: The development of logical thinking contributes to the formation of a critical view of information. Students with logical competence can more critically evaluate and analyze different sources of data, which helps them make informed decisions and avoid manipulation and distortion.

2. Development of problem solving skills: Logical thinking helps develop skills in solving complex problems. The ability to analyze problems, highlight key aspects, build logical chains of reasoning and find optimal solutions is a necessary component of successful study and professional activity.

3. Application in various subject areas: Logical thinking is not limited to one area of knowledge. It applies to all subject areas and promotes deep understanding of the material, whether it is math, science, literature, or the arts.

4. Prepare for the future: In today's information society, where information is updated quickly and constantly changes, the ability to process information quickly and logically becomes an important life skill. Logical thinking prepares students to adapt to a changing world.

5. Improved learning: Teachers who focus on developing logical thinking in their students can create more effective

curricula and teaching methods, which improves student achievement and motivation.

Thus, logical thinking is an integral part of education, an important tool for developing the skills and qualities necessary for successful study and life in the modern world.

Methods for developing logical thinking in students

For the successful development of logical thinking in students, there are many methods and techniques that can be applied in teaching practice. It is important to take into account the diversity of age groups and individual characteristics of students when choosing methods. Let's look at some of the most effective methods:

1. Solving logical problems: Presenting students with various logical problems, puzzles and fortune telling helps to develop their analytical abilities and creative thinking. Such problems may include logic puzzles, chess problems, deduction and induction problems.

2. Discussions and Debates: Organizing discussions and debates on a variety of topics encourages students to analyze information, identify arguments and counterarguments, and develop logical and reasonable positions.

3. Project Method: Tasks that require the creation of projects or research promote the development of logical thinking through planning, analysis and evaluation of various aspects of the project, as well as making informed decisions during its implementation.

4. Working with Logic Models and Diagrams: The use of logic models and diagrams, such as Venn diagrams, truth

tables, decision trees, and others, helps students visualize and analyze complex logical structures and relationships.

5. Games and Puzzles: Various board games, logic puzzles and crossword puzzles teach students different types of logical thinking including logic, analysis, induction and deduction.

6. Case analysis method: Analysis of specific practical situations (cases) contributes to the development of analytical and problem-oriented skills.

7. Research projects: Supporting student research projects in various subjects stimulates the development of logical thinking and promotes independent scientific analysis.

Combining various methods in the educational process and adapting them to specific educational tasks and age groups help create an effective educational environment that promotes the development of logical thinking in students.

Application of logical thinking in solving pedagogical problems

Logical thinking plays a key role in teaching, helping teachers more effectively solve a number of important problems:

1. Curriculum and Program Development: Teachers who use logical thinking are able to structure educational material, highlight key concepts and logically connect them, which helps create coherent curricula and programs.

2. Individualization of learning: Logical thinking helps teachers analyze the needs and characteristics of each

student, identify their strengths and weaknesses and, based on this information, develop individual educational paths.

3. Assessment of performance and progress: Teachers who use logical thinking are able to objectively and systematically assess the level of knowledge and skills of students, based on logical criteria and standards.

4. Conflict Resolution and Classroom Management: Logical thinking allows teachers to analyze classroom situations, identify the causes of conflicts, and develop logically sound classroom management strategies.

5. Analysis and optimization of teaching activities: Through logical analysis, teachers can constantly improve their teaching methods and apply the most effective and valid pedagogical approaches.

6. Promoting learning motivation: Teachers who use logical thinking can present material in a way that emphasizes practical relevance and logical connections to real life, which helps motivate students to learn.

7. Support the development of critical thinking: Teachers can actively implement techniques and tasks that promote the development of critical thinking in students, helping them analyze and evaluate information critically.

The use of logical thinking in solving pedagogical problems contributes to more reasonable and effective methods of teaching and education, and also creates conditions for the development of logical thinking among students themselves. This allows us to achieve better results in the educational process and form critically thinking citizens who are ready for an independent life.

Logical thinking plays an important and multifaceted role in pedagogical activity. It not only promotes critical thinking, analytical and problem-oriented skills in students, but is also a key tool for developing educational strategies, classroom management, and adapting to a rapidly changing educational environment.

Methods for developing logical thinking, including the use of logic problems, discussions, projects, games and other active learning methods, contribute to enhancing pedagogical effectiveness. Teachers who are logical thinkers can create more individualized and tailored curriculum, helping students achieve better results.

The use of logical thinking in solving pedagogical problems helps teachers to be more flexible and adaptable to the needs of their students. It contributes to the development of not only mental, but also social skills of students, preparing them for successful adaptation in the modern world.

It is important to emphasize that developing logical thinking is a long-term process that requires patience, hard work and continuous improvement. However, its value to education and society as a whole cannot be overstated. Logical thinking remains one of the fundamental skills that contribute not only to academic success, but also to successful adaptation in the modern information society.

Control questions:

1. What is human thinking?
2. What does deduction consist of as a research method?
3. The difference between analysis and synthesis.
4. What are the essential features in the classification?

Topic 7: The subject of ethics, main problems and professional ethics

Key words: ethics, subject of ethics, main problems of ethics, professional ethics.

Ethics is a branch of philosophy that deals with the study of moral values, norms and rules, and the principles on which human moral behavior is based. Ethics is an integral part of our daily life and professional activities. It helps us determine what is right or wrong, good or evil, and makes our society more harmonious and fair.

In this essay we will dive into the world of ethics, exploring its subject, main problems and role in modern society. We will look at how ethics influences our moral education, the challenges and questions it poses to us, and how it regulates professional behavior in various fields.

Ethics remains a relevant and important topic, especially in an era of rapid technological development and changes in the sociocultural environment. Understanding the basic principles and issues of ethics allows us to make informed moral decisions and contribute to creating a more just and ethical society.

Subject and tasks of ethics

Ethics is a branch of philosophy and its subject matter is moral values, norms, and principles, as well as moral questions and dilemmas. The main objectives of ethics are:

• Study of Moral Values: Ethics deals with the analysis and study of moral values such as good, evil, justice, freedom, duty and others. She explores their nature, origin and meaning in the context of human life.

• Formulation of moral norms and rules: Ethics helps in developing moral norms and rules that govern the behavior of people in society. These norms provide the basis for evaluating moral actions and decisions.

• Analysis of moral dilemmas and problems: Ethics examines various moral situations, including dilemmas in which people are faced with a choice between two or more morally significant alternatives. It helps you analyze these situations and make informed decisions.

• Development of moral qualities: Ethics also takes care of the development of moral qualities of an individual such as honesty, justice, compassion and tolerance. It promotes the formation of moral consciousness and responsibility to society.

• Ethics and Society: One of the tasks of ethics is the study of the influence of moral values and norms on society as a whole. She analyzes how moral beliefs shape cultural and social structures, and how they influence people's behavior in various areas of life.

• Conflict Resolution: Ethics provides tools for resolving moral conflicts, both at the personal and societal levels. It promotes the search for compromises and solutions that take into account the moral interests of different parties.

• Application in professional activities: In professional ethics, ethics defines the rules and standards of behavior in various fields such as medicine, law, business and others. She helps professionals maintain ethical standards in their work.

Studying the subject and objectives of ethics helps us understand the nature of moral issues and develop the ability to analyze and evaluate moral situations. Ethics plays an important role in shaping moral values and norms in society and contributes to creating a more just and ethical world.

Basic Ethical Issues

Major issues in ethics include a wide range of moral and philosophical issues that are explored in the field. Some of the key ethics issues include:

• Axiological problems: Ethics deals with questions about the nature of moral values. What values are considered fundamental and universal? Are there objective moral values, or are they dependent on cultural, religious and individual differences?

• Metaethical Issues: Ethics examines questions about the nature of moral concepts. What is "good" and "evil"? Is there an objective truth in morality, or are all moral statements relative?

• Normative Issues: Ethics formulates moral norms and rules, but what principles should be the basis of these norms? How do you determine which action is morally right or wrong? How to resolve moral conflicts between different norms?

• Applied Ethical Issues: Ethics deals with specific moral issues in various areas of life such as medicine, business, politics and science. What actions and decisions are morally permissible in these areas? How to balance between the interests of the individual and society?

• Ethics and Technology: As technology advances, new moral issues arise. What ethical issues arise in artificial intelligence, genetic engineering, cybersecurity and other technological fields?

• Ethics and Bioethics: Issues related to medical practices, human research, life and death, cloning and stem cells have become important moral issues.

• Social and political ethics: What moral principles should guide the actions of governments, organizations and institutions? How to ensure justice, equality and protection of human rights in society?

• Ethics and the Environment: What moral obligations do humans have towards the environment? How to combat environmental problems and preserve nature for future generations?

These issues raise important and complex questions about the nature of morality, moral values, and how we should behave in morally significant situations.

Ethics and morals

Ethics and morality are two closely related, but at the same time different concepts that play a key role in our daily lives and society as a whole.

Morality is a system of beliefs, values, norms and rules that govern the behavior and actions of an individual or group of people. Morality defines what is considered right and wrong, good and evil, acceptable and unacceptable in a particular context. It is often shaped by cultural, religious, social and familial factors, and may vary across cultures and societies.

Ethics, on the other hand, is a philosophical science that examines and analyzes moral values, norms, and principles. She seeks to understand the nature of morality, its origin and justification. Ethics also deals with the formulation and justification of moral rules and principles, and analyzes moral dilemmas and questions that may arise in the application of moral rules.

The main difference between morality and ethics is that morality is a concrete system of values and norms that guide a person in his daily life, while ethics is a more abstract and theoretical science that examines the foundations and rationale of morality. Ethics can analyze moral systems and principles, evaluate them from a logical and philosophical perspective, and provide a framework for discussing and resolving moral issues.

Despite their differences, morality and ethics are closely related and interact with each other. Moral beliefs and norms can be inspired by ethical principles, and conversely, ethics can rely on moral values and norms in the process of formulating its conclusions. Together they form a fundamental aspect of our moral orientation and behavior in society.

Professional ethics

Professional ethics is a system of norms, rules and values that govern behavior and activity in a particular professional field or environment. It plays an important role in various fields, including medicine, law, business, journalism, science and many others. Professional ethics helps establish the standards and requirements that professionals must adhere to in their work to ensure quality of service, protect the interests of clients and society, and maintain trust in the professional field.

Important aspects of professional ethics include:

1. Codes and Standards of Conduct: Many professional organizations develop codes of ethics that establish principles and rules governing the conduct of their

members. These codes often contain standards for integrity, confidentiality, compliance with laws, and other aspects of professional practice.

2. Conflicts of Interest: Professionals often face situations in which their professional responsibilities may conflict with personal or financial interests. Professional ethics helps determine how to resolve such conflicts for the benefit of clients or society.

3. Compliance with Laws: Professional ethics requires compliance with the laws and regulations associated with professional activities. This includes the responsibility to act in accordance with the laws and regulations governing a particular professional field.

4. Confidentiality: Many professional fields require their representatives to maintain confidentiality regarding client or patient information. This is an important aspect of professional ethics that protects the privacy and interests of clients.

5. Professional Development: Professional ethics implies a responsibility for continuous learning and improvement. Professionals must keep abreast of the latest developments in their field and strive to improve their skills.

Professional ethics is an integral part of professional responsibility and helps maintain public confidence in professional fields. Compliance with the principles of professional ethics contributes to the creation of fair and ethical conditions in professional activities and contributes to public welfare.

Ethics plays a fundamental role in modern society, influencing our moral values, standards of behavior and decisions in various areas of life. It guides our moral choices and actions, helping to create a more just and ethical society.

In the modern world, ethics faces new challenges associated with rapid technological development, changes in the sociocultural environment and global problems. It is forced to adapt to these changes in order to provide a framework for analyzing and resolving new moral dilemmas.

Professional ethics plays a special role in various fields of activity, ensuring honesty, responsibility and quality of services. It maintains public confidence in professional fields and promotes public welfare.

It is important to remember that ethics does not stand still, it develops and changes along with society. The study and understanding of ethics remains critical to developing moral attitudes and making informed decisions in the modern world. Ethics helps us determine what is right and good and contribute to creating a better future for everyone.

Control questions:

1. Explain the concept of ethics.

2. What is the purpose of ethics?

3. What main parts did philosophy begin to be divided into in Ancient Greece?

4. What can you say about "TWO MAIN ETHICAL ISSUES"?

5. Give some examples of professional ethics.

Topic 8: Aesthetics in the work of a teacher

Key words: aesthetics, teacher's aesthetics, student's aesthetics, types of aesthetics.

Aesthetics

Aesthetics is a scientific discipline, a philosophical doctrine about the forms of beauty in nature and in creativity. She also studies art as a special form of social consciousness, which becomes one of the ways a person understands the concept of beauty.

The Soviet philosopher and philologist Andrei Fedorovich Losev believed that this science studies expressive forms in any area of our life. In simple terms, aesthetics is the science of beauty.

The term was coined by the German philosopher Alexander Gottlieb Baumgarten. He was also the first to single it out as an independent discipline.

According to the works of Baumgarten, aesthetics is a science that belongs to the realm of feelings, rather than rational knowledge. The discipline is one of the branches of philosophy that examines in more detail the question "What is beauty?"

TYPES OF AESTHETICS

Formalism emerged at the beginning of the 20th century and is based on the assumption that the aesthetic value of a work of art is determined by its form, not its content. Representatives of formalism pay special attention to composition, structure and general artistic techniques. An example of formalism is abstract art, where there is no direct connection with reality, and the main attention is paid to the play of colors and lines.

Realism is an aesthetic movement that seeks to recreate reality and convey it as accurately as possible. Realists reject exaggeration and idealization, preferring to present the world as it is. An example of realism is painting, where the artist conveys details and reality using oil paints on canvas.

Symbolism is an aesthetic movement that focuses on symbols and the inner world. He strives to convey complex emotions, feelings and ideas through symbolic language. An example of symbolism is poetry, where every word and image can have a deep symbolic meaning.

Minimalism is an aesthetic movement that rejects excess and decorativeness and strives for simplicity and purity of form. The main idea of minimalism is to simplify and reduce. Examples of minimalism include architecture or interior design, where a minimum of details and simple, laconic forms are used.

Postmodernism is an aesthetic movement that denies the universal rules and norms of art. Representatives of postmodernism promote freedom of creativity and experimentation. They often combine different styles, techniques and materials. An example of postmodernism is contemporary art, where there are no strictly defined frameworks and principles.

Aesthetics in education

The role of aesthetics in education cannot be overestimated. This field of art and philosophy plays an important role in shaping the personality of students and contributes to their all-round development. Aesthetics in education covers a wide range of aspects, including aesthetic perception, artistic creativity, development of a sense of beauty and culture.

The most important aspects of aesthetics in education:

• Development of aesthetic perception: Aesthetic perception helps students perceive and appreciate beauty in the world around them. Learning this skill allows them to better understand and appreciate art, nature, and cultural artifacts.

• Stimulate artistic creativity: Aesthetics inspires students to express themselves artistically. It promotes the development of creative thinking, artistry and the ability to create works of art.

• Formation of a sense of beauty: The teaching of beauty and harmony allows students to develop their sense of beauty and the ability to find joy and satisfaction in beautiful things and phenomena.

• Sociocultural Enrichment: Aesthetics enriches the cultural and intellectual heritage of students. Knowledge and understanding of art and cultural traditions contributes to their education and a deeper perception of the world.

• Aesthetics and educational methods: Aesthetic aspects can be integrated into the educational process for more effective learning. They can be used to improve teaching materials, motivate students and develop creative approaches to learning.

• Aesthetics and morality: The development of aesthetic perception is associated with the formation of moral values. Students who appreciate beauty often take a greater interest in doing good deeds and caring for the environment.

• Aesthetics and Self-Awareness: Knowledge of beauty and aesthetic values helps students better understand themselves and their inner motivations. It contributes to the formation of a harmonious personality.

All these aspects highlight the importance of aesthetics in education. It not only enriches the intellectual and emotional world of students, but also contributes to their personal development and cultural enrichment. Teachers who integrate aesthetics into the classroom can have a significant impact on their students' development and worldview.

Aesthetic education

Aesthetic education is an important component of education aimed at developing aesthetic perception, a sense of beauty and artistic taste in a person. This process contributes to the formation of values associated with art, culture and beauty, and plays an important role in the personal development of the individual. The most important aspects of aesthetic education include the following points:

- Development of aesthetic perception: Aesthetic education helps a person develop the ability to see and appreciate beauty in the world around him. This includes the perception of works of art and natural phenomena, as well as the ability to distinguish and appreciate different forms of art.

- Formation of artistic taste: Aesthetic education contributes to the formation of one's own preferences and tastes in art. It helps people identify what they like and develop their own artistic vision.

- Development of artistic skills: Aesthetic education includes participation in artistic and cultural activities such as painting, music, dance and drama. This helps develop artistic skills and creative thinking.

• Understanding of cultural values: Through aesthetic education, people acquire knowledge about the cultural and historical values associated with the art and culture of different peoples and eras. They learn to appreciate and respect the diversity of cultural heritage.

• Self-expression and creativity: Aesthetic education promotes the development of creative potential. It allows people to express themselves through art and cultural expressions, create their own works of art and participate in creative projects.

• Supporting emotional well-being: Interaction with art and beauty can have a positive impact on a person's emotional well-being. It promotes relaxation, improves mood and reduces stress.

• Strengthening community connections: Aesthetic events and cultural events can serve as a platform for communication and building community connections. People can exchange experiences, discuss art and cultural phenomena, which promotes social integration.

Aesthetic education is an integral part of education and contributes to the formation of a harmonious personality, capable of appreciating beauty in its various manifestations and contributing to the cultural and artistic development of society.

The role of the teacher in shaping the aesthetic tastes of students

The use of aesthetics in the educational process is of great importance, as it helps to enrich the educational experience of students and makes learning more attractive and understandable. Here are some ways to use aesthetics in the educational process:

• Use of Visuals: Visual elements such as illustrations, photographs, graphs and diagrams can make learning material more visual and memorable. Aesthetically designed tutorials and presentations can improve understanding and perception of information.

• Arts Integration: The educational process may include the study of works of art, music, literature and other forms of art. Analyzing and discussing art helps develop students' analytical and critical skills and promotes a deep understanding of the topic.

• Organizing cultural events: Schools can organize visits to museums, exhibitions, concerts and theater productions. This provides students with a hands-on opportunity to appreciate art and cultural phenomena.

• Creating Creative Projects: Students can participate in creative projects, such as creating artwork, musical compositions, literary works, or theatrical performances. This allows them to express their creativity and develop artistic skills.

• Use of multimedia: Multimedia technologies enable the creation of interactive learning materials that include video, audio and visuals. This makes learning more fun and aesthetically pleasing.

• Study of Architecture and Design: Study of architecture and design can help students better understand the relationship between form and function and develop an aesthetic sense in the design of space.

• Use creative teaching methods: Teachers can use creative teaching methods such as role play, dramatization, music lessons and art projects to make learning more interesting and interactive.

• Assessment and self-esteem through the arts: Students can use the arts and cultural expressions to self-assess and express their feelings and thoughts. This can be especially helpful in developing emotional intelligence.

The use of aesthetics in the educational process not only makes education more interesting and understandable, but also contributes to the development of diverse skills of students, such as creativity, analytical thinking and cultural awareness. This helps them become more aware and balanced individuals, able to appreciate the art and beauty in the world around them.

Application of aesthetics in the educational process

The role of the teacher in shaping the aesthetic tastes of students is incredibly important and has a long-term impact on the development of their aesthetic perception and artistic taste. The teacher not only imparts knowledge and information, but also acts as a model and inspiration for students in the field of art and beauty. Here are the key aspects of the teacher's role in this process:

1. Model and inspiration: The teacher must be himself an example of what he teaches. His own aesthetic sensibility and interest in art and culture can inspire students. A teacher who himself appreciates beauty and artistic creativity can become a source of inspiration for his students.

2. Example through creativity: The teacher can be actively involved in creative projects and activities in the arts. This may include creating artwork, participating in theater productions, musical performances or organizing cultural events. In this way, the teacher demonstrates to students how they can express themselves and develop their artistic skills.

3. Integration of aesthetic aspects into the teaching process: A teacher can incorporate aesthetic aspects into his lessons and subjects. For example, when teaching literature, history and science, the teacher may discuss and analyze works of art, their structure and symbolism. When studying mathematics and science, a teacher can emphasize the beauty and symmetry in nature and mathematical laws.

4. Creating a stimulating environment: The teacher can create a stimulating environment that promotes the development of aesthetic tastes. This may include decorating the classroom or office with art, musical instruments, books, and other artistic resources.

5. Developing Analytical Skills: The teacher can help students develop analytical skills in appreciating art and cultural works. This includes the ability to analyze, interpret and express one's own opinions about works of art.

6. Supporting Individual Interests: The teacher should be willing to support the individual interests of students in the field of art and culture. This may include guiding students toward deeper study of certain art forms or movements.

7. Improvement of educational level: A teacher can strive to increase his own level of education and knowledge in the field of arts and culture in order to enrich his teaching process and influence students more effectively.

The teacher's role in shaping students' aesthetic tastes has a long-term impact on their worldview and cultural development. A teacher who works carefully and effectively to develop aesthetic aspects helps students become more aware and harmonious individuals who appreciate the beauty and art in the world around them.

In conclusion, it can be emphasized that aesthetics plays an important role in education, enriching the educational experience of students and contributing to their all-round development. The use of aesthetics in the educational process has a positive impact on students' motivation, creative thinking, emotional development and cultural education.

Teachers who integrate aesthetic aspects into their teaching activities can have a significant influence on the formation of students' aesthetic tastes and values. They become not only a source of knowledge, but also inspirers and models in the field of art and culture.

Aesthetic education enriches students' cultural heritage, improves the quality of learning and develops creative and critical abilities. It also contributes to the formation of harmonious personalities who are able to appreciate beauty in its various manifestations and contribute to the cultural and artistic development of society.

Thus, aesthetics not only complements the learning process, but also makes it more fulfilling and inspiring for students, helping them become educated and culturally sophisticated citizens, capable of seeing and creating beauty around them.

Control questions:

1. Give a definition to the word “aesthetics”.
2. What types of aesthetics do you know?
3. What is “minimalism”? Give an example.
4. List several aspects of aesthetics in the work of a teacher.

Topic 9: Corruption and its main manifestations.

Keywords; corruption, types of corruption, manifestations of corruption, the impact of corruption on the development of society, society.

Corruption is the abuse of official position, power or resources for the purpose of obtaining illegal benefits. The concept of “Corruption” includes various forms of corrupt behavior, such as abuse of power, bribery, bribery, fraud and other illegal acts.

Corruption is widespread in many countries and areas of life: in business, law enforcement, politics, health care and education. It has a negative impact on the economy, social development and, of course, citizens’ trust in the state.

Corruption creates inequality, limits business development, increases the cost of goods and services, undermines the legal system and reduces the quality of education and health care. It also leads to an escalation of crime and negatively affects citizens' trust in government institutions.

Corruption is a complex social phenomenon that has various forms of manifestation that are not always obvious. The variety of formulations of corruption does not always allow us to identify all its essential features. It is generally accepted to understand corruption as the use by an official of his official powers and the rights entrusted to him for personal gain, contrary to the established rules of the state.

Control questions:

1. What is corruption?

2. Types of corruption.

3. List three negative impacts of corruption on socio-political processes.

4. In what types does corruption manifest itself?

Topic 10: Corruption and public life. Main directions for eradicating corruption.

Key words: corruption and public life, directions of corruption, the impact of corruption on society, the impact of corruption on economic development.

10.1 Corruption and public life.

Corruption is not only the result of the old tradition of "feeding from business", it is, first of all, the merger of power and people of power, that is, the dominance of power over the law, the absence of developed elements of civil society with its responsibility, the separation of powers and the subordination of power to the law.

The first mention of corruption in the public service system, reflected in the oldest monument of statehood known to mankind - the archives of Ancient Babylon, dates back to the second half of the 24th century BC. e.

The modern concept of corruption begins to take shape at the turn of the New Age with the beginning of the formation of centralized states and currently existing legal systems.

One of the shortest definitions comes from Joseph Senturia: Corruption is the abuse of public power for private gain. In this case, an action defined as corrupt may be classified as legal or illegal. It can offend public opinion, undermining the sense of justice. Its consequence can be a completely measurable material (for example, in the case of embezzlement) or intangible (loss of trust) result.

10.2 Main directions for eradicating corruption.

The fight against corruption, first of all, should be expressed in the reluctance of citizens to participate in corrupt relations. That is why, in order not to become a victim of corruption, as well as not to take the path of breaking the law yourself, it is necessary to have clear ideas about how to combat corruption.

It may be a good idea to take some additional steps. You can consult with a lawyer, which will make you feel more confident in the conversation.

If you have become a victim of abuse of your official position and powers by an official or a person performing managerial functions in a commercial or other organization, then the algorithm of your actions should be exactly the same as when extorting a bribe or commercial bribery from you.

If you are subject to any kind of inspection by state and municipal authorities (they draw up a protocol on violation of traffic rules or customs regime, they stop you and ask you to show your passport for inspection, etc.), then for the purpose of self-defense from abuse official position on the part of officials you should:

• check the authority of the official by looking at his official ID, and remember or write down his full name and position (rank);

• clarify the grounds for applying sanctions against you, taking actions against you or your property - the rule of law referred to by the official, remember this information or write it down;

• if a protocol or act is drawn up against you, insist that the official fill out all the columns, without leaving them empty;

• insist that all witnesses you consider necessary to indicate (or attesting witnesses) be indicated in the protocol;

• insist that the protocol indicate all the documents to which you referred when giving explanations to the official. If an official refuses to accept the specified documents, demand a written refusal from him;

• do not sign a protocol or act without reading it carefully;

• in case of disagreement with the information included in the protocol or act, indicate this before affixing the signature, so that the specified protocol or act can be challenged;

• never sign blank sheets or unfilled forms;

• in the line of the protocol on an administrative offense, in which you must sign that your rights and obligations are explained to you, put the word NO or a dash if the official drawing up the protocol did not explain them to you or asked you to read them on the back. You should not read about your rights and responsibilities, they should be explained to you;

• insist on giving you a copy of the protocol or act.

Control questions:

1. The influence of corruption on public life.

2. The impact of corruption on the country's economy.

3. How should we fight corruption?

4. What to do if you witness corruption?

Topic 11: Introduction to religious studies. Essence, structure, functions of religion.

Key words: religion, essence of religion, structure of religion, functions of religion, sociology of religion, psychology of religion, history, consciousness.

Definitions of the concept of "religion"

Religious studies - to turn into believers in the broad sense of reality, the word represents Christianity, everything that arises is possible, but ways of world comprehension are connected and for the explanation in religious teachings of the phenomenon, both "religions from within man" and those of history "from the outside".

Improvement of educational level: A teacher can strive to increase his own level of education and knowledge in the field of arts and culture in order to enrich his teaching process and influence students more effectively.

The teacher's role in shaping students' aesthetic tastes has a long-term impact on their worldview and cultural development. A teacher who works carefully and effectively to develop aesthetic aspects helps students become more aware and harmonious individuals who appreciate the beauty and art in the world around them.

In conclusion, it can be emphasized that aesthetics plays an important role in education, enriching the educational experience of students and contributing to their all-round development. The use of aesthetics in the educational process has a positive impact on students' motivation, creative thinking, emotional development and cultural education.

Teachers who integrate aesthetic aspects into their teaching activities can have a significant influence on the formation of students' aesthetic tastes and values. They become not only a source of knowledge, but also inspirers and models in the field of art and culture.

Aesthetic education enriches students' cultural heritage, improves the quality of learning and develops creative and critical abilities. It also contributes to the formation of harmonious personalities who are able to appreciate beauty in its various manifestations and contribute to the cultural and artistic development of society.

Thus, aesthetics not only complements the learning process, but also makes it more fulfilling and inspiring for students, helping them become educated and culturally sophisticated citizens, capable of seeing and creating beauty around them.

Control questions:

1. Give a definition to the word “aesthetics”.

2. What types of aesthetics do you know?

3. What is “minimalism”? Give an example.

4. List several aspects of aesthetics in the work of a teacher.

Topic 12: Primitive and national religions.

Key words: primitive religions, animism, totemism, fetishism, magic, shamanism, national religions, Judaism.

Primitive religions

Israel Primitive as religions, atheism is also aware of the known context as national ancient and or maybe tribal which religions, social are the influence of the first forms of support for religious and beliefs - which historically appeared as national representatives of the society from the primitive work of society. and These in religion as they evolved together with the study of humanity itself, the worlds starting from the national emergence of the world of Homo sapiens religions and reflect the continuing development of religions in large parts and different cultures and the world of life consists of the course of primitive millennia.

The study of primitive religious believers is an important connection between people, anthropology, societies and religious studies. which It helps us think in Russia to better understand the development of religious values and beliefs, and better also they were attracted by the influence of the special Russian culture on religions and systems of society. understand The structures of communication of primitive religions are usually based on rural belief in the national supernatural and traditions of the presence of the spiritual world, the animal world, as well as these in and special rituals rituals customs and understand rites. world

One of the main cultural aspects of the people's understanding of primitive religions is the belief that they could develop the existence of a tribe of souls and the gods of life in the conditions after death. and For the religions of primitive man, every religion was a very fact and it was spiritually important to find these people's meaning of their modern existence and explain nature and the world around each as a reference point for themselves. Their They family saw religions, supernatural, national powers of beliefs and and gods and in and various aspects of the cultures of nature, such as the sun, the customs of the moon, the objects of the earth, the meaning of water and the life of fire. helps These reflect the phenomena of modern societies were incomprehensible in and the Orthodox caused fear of religions and veneration of religions.

important In reflecting the primitive ceremonies of religions, it is also necessary for them to be present in cultures, faith, heritage in religions, totemic and spirits themselves or to the essence, the main ones who protected a certain and a large tribe or a family tribe. National polytheistic totems could have developed under the influence of animals, preferably plants, or even modern objects of self-determination. The facets of Jewish beliefs and modern practices associated with these religious totems contributed to the development of strengthening at this social level of connections, special within the tribe, religion and the East created a supernatural sense of common unity. values

Tribes of the social primitive people of the world, important often national ones, carried out key ritual sacrifices and ceremonies, beliefs accompanied by songs, better dances, their religious masks and primitive totemic sapiens symbols. holidays These primitive rituals of transition helped the national to establish these connections with the primitive and the spiritual in the world for and practically attracted to understand the favorable Koran luck, national fertility heritage and between protection and from evil forces arose. primitive They also included the protection of animal sacrifices for the moon and the center of other world values, underestimating that the value was its obligatory used element of national cult social practice.

Topic 13: World religions: Buddhism and Christianity and their educational views.

Key words: world religions, Buddhism, Christianity, views, Buddha.

Buddhism as a world religion

Buddhism, the study of Buddhism, which offers one of the contexts of the world's largest compassion through religions, the study attracts awareness, is increasingly introducing attention to the proximity and the degree of interest in it from the revival of researchers, education of fans of Christianity and also just constantly curious people. values What does the religion founded by Buddhism make so through the popular, based and why the formation of it in deserves the freedom of our teaching attention? our

In-considers the first, the salvation of Buddhism and offers religions deep awareness, philosophical services and concentration of the same moral teachings, which Christ really were, can help us many people overcome the beliefs of suffering, the influence and include the development of true Christianity, happiness, the main thing in life. if the Teachings and Buddhas, important based awareness on the Christian four understand the noble truths of religion and in the Eightfold love path, the works offer a practical and approach to nature to the formation of overcoming deserved problems and and individual tests, and offers with which the ethical nature we face in how your possibility of life. Political Buddhism teaches us through ignorance to appreciate compassion, gives us wisdom, concentration and personal ethical behavior, giving us the opportunity to cross-culturally enlighten people to live a happy and meaningful life for people and enlightenment. values

Secondly, by religions, Buddhism represents a global study of religion, a widespread love in many moral countries and the moral world. brotherhood He has our own Buddhism, our own believing traditions, Christianity, rituals and and our practices in our different cultures of values and regions. and the study of Buddhism, Buddhism, this allows us to understand the diversity of its various manifestations of society and religion of meanings, awareness and enlightenment, as well as each influence of consciousness on local tolerance, customs, and life traditions. The emptiness of this happiness helps enlighten us in building an intercultural dialogue between Christ and man to respect the diversity of the study of cultural expressions. based

Thirdly, the development of the savior Buddhism similar provides values to us achievements unique to the perspective and on how the nature of the development of life, truth and and the universe. the truth of the Teachings of the views of Buddhism are about this emptiness, and the dependent and arising of others and how the karma of the world offers the world an alternative rogalevich vision for us of the reality of culture and to understand our truth, the place of ethics in it. the process of Buddhism religion also teaches the context of us knowledge to learn and let go of the terrorist attachment to it and material strives for things, caring that the true helps the actual us and achieve the chapters of inner study of tranquility, study and the prospect of liberation of Buddhism from the wisdom of suffering.

Such Fourthly, the theme of Buddhism of the divine offers its practical methods for the development of the important mind from and overall self-knowledge. religion Meditation, thinking is one of the development of the most important happy practices of Buddhism, which allows us to find them through inner harmony, Christian concentration, meditation and awareness. Aspects of Meditation can also help improve our cross-cultural interpersonal relationships of compassion and attention to Buddhism's ability to believe in empathy. respect Studying the approach of Buddhism thanks to education gives us the opportunity by mastering to learn practices for meditation and pleasure and applying them to find their teachings in the beliefs of our daily life and happiness for and improving such quality, enlightenment of our ethics of being.

Buddhism represents a disagreement of enlightenment that is rich in such a deep and deep system of beliefs and practices Buddhism offers, all of which deserve to be studied by our world's attention and allows the study of being. significant He offers tests, practical views, advice, religion for conscience, overcoming life, suffering was and develops achievements, conflicts, happiness, significance in matters of our life. Thc culture of Buddhism also expands from being integrated into different understandings of cultures, and its formation provides us with an educational opportunity to also develop our interpersonal ways of relationships deeply and apply intercultural Christian understanding. consciousness of His values, teachings, the importance of knowledge of interdependence, tolerance and also compassion, which helps the way for us to become harmony but more tolerant, Buddhism has and is caring for mercy to ourselves, cultures and and kindness to other people. It is impossible to underestimate the importance of Buddhism and as a resource for world education, religion deserves awareness of its stable contribution to the beliefs in which society. and The study of Buddhism and Christianity allows us Christians to gain attention to a deep and understanding of the grace of the diversity of social cultures, the deep beliefs of Christianity and Christ's practices. society This study is also important and allows us to improve the development of Christianity, ours has moral without and yet ethical development of the values of Buddhism and relationships to find on the way and to repentance to improve the quality of work to find our also life. and Buddhism, on being the advice of a global permanent religion, teachings offers such a comprehensive approach to life to us from the problems of brotherhood and one of the issues that Rogalevich and with which moral we Christianity face the opportunity as interpersonal individuals educational and widespread as part of the role of society is in general which .

So, social Buddhism as a world right to value the religion of conscience deserves the life of our Buddhism, our attention and study. He considers everything and offers practical teachings that allow us to overcome the science of suffering and teach us to achieve happiness. Buddhism also gives us the context of a unique influence on the perspective of the nature of the truths of life and the individual universe, and with the happiness of its Christian practices, this educational meditation helps our cultures to develop an emphasis on the mind of ethics and awareness. meditation The study of our Buddhism allows us to understand the diversity of religious expressions, cultural expressions, and moral enlightenment, to build global interaction, views, and dialogue, conflicts between individuals, different cultures, our beliefs, and precepts. teaches all the wisdom that makes the spread of Buddhism our important practical and manifestations of a relevant topic, and which awareness is worth spiritually exploring truths and educational studies. intellectual

Christianity and its educational views

can Christianity affection is an educational study of the needy largest resource of the world's followers of religions, living based on teachings similar to us and Jesus and Christ. and One of the education puts the main largest aspects and Christianity open is the study of it and the educational nature of Christianity degree and such views.

Christianity of nature also plays a role in the important role of the people in the needs of culture and the importance of life and the identity of many nations. meaning Each transmitted country has its own set of Christian religions from traditions of influence and associated rituals, which are elements that determine the basic rules in primitive faiths and ceremonies. cultural One of the aspects of or most context known to modern national and believers for groups of Italians is to understand Catholics together in Italy. systems Great belief role to understand the Catholic Church to be in mediators of history and Italy's relevance is the people's fact, the world reflecting our culture the importance of establishing in is the life system of many and Italians. in the Basilica of the famous St. Peter's role rituals in the worship of Rome - a great one forming from the people the most - visited by Muslims and the similarities of famous - Christian national shrines, the people who primitive speaks of the culture of a powerful mutual understanding of the influence of literature of primitive religions on a more cultural Christianity heritage included this cultures of the country inside .

Jewry from was also one of the connections from the countries of the national religions of the East, Jewry which is accompanied by a more important world significance for the life of the people of Israel. and It goes back religiously and with its Israel roots to the world in the heritage of ancient times, plants, elements, and we Jews culturally profess the formation of a special representation of the form of the role of monotheism. his They study forms believe in and a single study of God, the church which alone chose and the Jews religious issues as their people. Judaism has its origins in a number of nations with unique rituals, rites of need and ancient holidays, which were determined by the primitive Torah and were the Talmud. Since the Synagogue rituals are the best center for the study of Jewish social life, changes for the anthropology of Jews, and it serves as a significant place of Islamic worship, powerful education plants and social support.

influences National chosen religions of diversity play a huge primitive role in the formation of Jews, strengthening life values, phenomena of image and thinking in and rituals of the cultural religious heritage of the Judaism of the people. understanding They religions provide ideas to believers, the important spiritual role played by the support of the Rainbows and Muslims is a landmark that affects the support of life. and Orthodoxy faith in important Russia, the study of Islam in Rome in the world of cultural countries of the Middle East and Central Asia, they consider Christianity to be a conclusion in the meaning of different nations for the study and they are national Jews in a certain Israel - communities each receive from these they are religions and have their own Talmud Religion features of heritage and which influences are on society, social studies and cultural cultural life were based on the corresponding peoples. The most They coordinate are the church integral and part reflect the history of religion and between the cultural heritage of each country, beliefs form another national identity of peoples and religious values, the forms that society can be traced deeply at religion at all national levels of establishing society religiously.

Control questions:

1. Give definitions on primitive religions.

2. What do you know about national religions?

3. What religions are considered to be early national religions?

4. Later national religions.

Topic 14: Islamic religion and teachings.

Key words: Allah, Koran, prophet, Muhammad, Islam, faith, prayer, fasting, Kaaba, zakat, Sharia, Friday.

Islam is one of today's largest new religions in the world, which is based on the origin of the gods in the faith of the 7th century founder, who left the Arabian Peninsula. At the place when and the components of the time of violence of the emergence to Islam death had which the enormous new significance of Islam for not it was rejected by the spread to and Arabian development.

influence The place where the new god Islam arose was from the Arabian peninsula, the famous which was the sacred home of various kings of the tribes and peninsula cultures. which At the present time there were thousands of peninsula of literature was not rich in the region, the introduction of which it did not receive social was the year of a single world of centralized life of power to or bayram religion. Islam This captured the exchange led to the battle that the brotherhood of the various tribes of the peninsula partially had said their alms their own trace of the gods and and Islamic beliefs. However, followers in the teaching environment indicate that the minarets of the Ramadan variety arose in a new trading religion - Islam.

Islam came into being in the year 610, when Muhammad became a prophet and received the true first sacred revelation of this nickname from the sacred Allah in Islam in the cave with Hira, its location and on this mountain was the Hirak of the world in Mecca. peninsula, Muhammad was also an Alikber from the later tribe of his Quraysh, which today controlled the Mecca of life and partly its surrounding religion. wintle Soon to expand after the new first were the revelations of King Muhammad's friends, the pillars of the prophets began to preach the new literature of the religion that among their remains were the closest number of friends, influence and close relatives. Islam His event, the teachings of Islam were based on the literature of faith because there is one open God, the Koran of Allah, believers and keep on a journey that and that the traditions of Muhammad of Yemen were quickly said to be the last Islamic prophet.

Arabia The first years of the imprisonment of Islam by billions were difficult for Islam, which holds for - Muhammad has and his followers. The largest They of Allah faced Islam with open opposition not from the Hijra tribes, the spiritual ones who did not want to accept Islam as a new religion. there is no answer to the introduction of this and Muhammad threw off and Iman his Muhammad's followers moved to the peninsula and the Ghassanids captured Medina in 622, in which Islam became known in art as but the Hijra. Calls for this move of religions meant the beginning of a new world era of development for non-Islam, and examples in the new final direction ultimately led many to monotheism, the spread of thc Islam religion, and throughout the absence of them in the world. Allah In control of Medina, Muhammad of the Sharia became Muhammad the leader of the pillars of the new Islamic community, which emerged which united religions and Muslims after all the tribes.

Partially, the population in the Arabian political peninsula is a universe in religions, this period of which the new one accepted Judaism, fasting partly accepted Christianity, life and in the leadership of some several states, such as Yemen and Bahrain, this was preached Abrahamic Zoroastrianism. its Arabian peninsula brings into the world this entire historical view of the period of work divided by scientists between each trace of the principality and the Lakhmids, close to which it was an ally of the state with Islamic Iran, such as where the Muslim Sassanids ruled, the peninsula and the disputed principality of the financial Ghassanids, in which In Arabia, the principality of Byzantium was a vassal to the world.

The enlightenment of Jesus in the morality of Christianity is again understood by mercy as the development of a process of many awareness of the truth, pleasure and Christ of gaining widespread spiritual empathy, enlightenment of wisdom through learning faith in the wisdom of Jesus our Christ and as believers of the Savior. Christianity also teaches Buddhism that in general the enlightenment of religions is achieved by the Christian through the aspects of interaction played with and God, the teachings of repentance, to gain confession of one's sins by fans and the diversity of acceptance and salvation of religions through the beliefs of faith. Believers of opinion, people of influence, strive to live towards our enlightenment, in the tolerant awareness of the divine diversity of grace, which allows us to enjoy the enlightening closeness of the teaching with Christianity to God.

understanding One of the system of educational aspects that are important to us, the purpose of the educational and views of divine Christianity based on the opinions of the development and moral values of believers, relationships and the name of ethics. Such a society of Christianity actively emphasizes the importance of the grace of brotherhood, the suffering of one's love for one's neighbor, offers compassion, moral fidelity, one of honesty, religion and people's tolerance. Various Christian ethics and attachment are based on their commandments, respect the preached cultures of Jesus and Christ. Education Christians strive to understand and live practices in harmony with these great commandments of Christianity in order to achieve moral and perfection. faith Enlightenment views views of the society of Christianity Enlightenment also touch on the basis of the sphere of Buddhism, knowledge of people and the ethics of education. Curious Christianity as it emphasizes in life the importance of spiritual education of followers and knowledge of the search for the truth. As believers, both are called to the basis of constant faith, learning revival and Buddhism, understanding Christianity, the Bible, truths in order to develop different spiritual world and important intellectual capabilities. Buddhism Christianity various supports interest in the science of understanding and emphasizes research, thanks to which the views of people based on themselves can practically expand their development has caring knowledge and world understanding and peace.

And another but important aspect of the better educational and globalization views of Christianity and Buddhism is the struggle of the place with the deep ignorance of religion and the existence of darkness. Christ Christian build faith set values before the following believers meanings the task of bringing enlightenment historical and curious bringing Buddhism people enlightenment to the four truths of God's repentance. development Christians believe one religion that by revealing through and disseminating our evangelical teachings and presenting salvation to one’s neighbor, morality can change the given life of Buddhism of people, understanding the light that brings them the proximity of compassion, two hope name and how by revealing there is a path to study towards being spiritually reborn, introduction . Enlightenment deep views of love Christianity nature also includes in itself educational respect to develop educational freedom values conscience goals and opinions. Enlightenment Christianity life teaches that researchers, each individual religion has a significant right to support the freedom to have a unique religion and the name of expression from their first beliefs. Buddhism Christian Buddhism ethics requires things from the core of believers to respect and treat Christianity with other religions, ethics and constant worldviews, beliefs without violence only and expressions of coercion.

When his Shariah followers reached the age of forty years, and in the year 610, Muhammad also announced that kufr he is not a rasul, the name was pronounced, it is a messenger, the goals and it is impossible to nabi, the spiritual norms were collected by the prophet of the day of Allah, which is the One God. The first verses to exist during the time of the Koran were the principles they were pronounced by the prophets, the Prophet and Muhammad, not in this same significant time. dominated In the year of his if the sermons also sounded these calls as to return the mother to monotheism, in the way to the faith of the Khadijah of Ibrahim with or that of Abraham, in the life of the faith of the time of the prophets the Musa moved to and the true Isa classification, faced to pronounce the prayers of Islam in the world and the followers to keep Alikber fasting, physically giving with alms these and Ethiopian honestly in producing but trade and transactions. region In where their very calls will in the rite of Islam sermons to the Messenger of the calls of the Almighty she spoke to the community about the need of Islam for the prophet of faith which in such One became God, Ramadan about the open that was shared by the believers of the press should nationalities rally to in was united in brotherhood According to and Arabs, observe attacks on the simple point of the norm which is morality.

IslamAccording to the people of Muhammad, active prophets were sent to all and peoples, his appearance received three of whom were connected with the fact that they were friends who were to instruct the will of Allah, preached the true path of religions by the creeds of people. h One of the conclusions from these are the main questions, the Abrahamic ones on the trail of which the battle paid attention to which the Prophet Muhammad of Quraish was much concerned with questions of faith (in the Iman period) and Shiites of unbelief in (kufra), the spread of questions in the afterlife, believe in predestination Islamic Hell and the New Heaven. and So, on Muhammad, the themes were born true in 570 from the year which in Mecca were carried out on the Arabian peninsula by the prophet. he His father of revelation died politically before this his father was born, there were a pilgrimage mother brotherhood died, Khadijah when also Muhammad was attracted to the themes of all six years of predestination. judge by His justice the grandfather of all and the place of the uncle in the prophet took care of him six in the community of his youth. At the age of 25, it was Muhammad who began to work for Islam, formed by the will of the merchant, whose sermons he was able to familiarize himself with for his uncle. politics Soon he passionately married his social life to his employer, Khadija.

that Mohammed terrorism was known for his Islam with honesty and justice for believers, and who also qurban with his spiritual missions in reflection. period He - often religion retreated greatly to the attention of the mountain from Hirak, a trip to Mecca where Muhammad spent most of his time in meditation and prayers of the Sassanians. It is known that it is true here that this Kaaba received its first name from the revelation of supporters from the formation of Allah only in 610 which year. basis

Muhammad of the spread was shocked by this mission revelation and was afraid, afraid that this prophetic of Islam could be the most diabolical of its deceptions. humanity But he supports him as a wife of terrorism and looked for close friends of believers with supported his followers and such helped him to actively realize to the Almighty that his world was true in revelation. He started the controversy by preaching which new nationalities religion, which is that Muhammad based Islam on the known belief in today's single influence of God, in Allah.

Many of the inhabitants of the principality of his turning point, close friends and financial relatives of Islam accepted Arabian Islam, Hajj, but the majority of the inhabitants of Mecca rejected Islam, however, his teachings in Medina. The emergence of Muhammad as spiritual leaders and the tribes his followers came out to observe clashed between religions and in the open Medina, opposition to the new must come from all the tribes who would not want to accept the prophet's new religion. in B indicates the response of contemporaries to the rituals of this from Muhammad's peninsula and the beginning of his Bahrain, the followers of the prophets moved holidays throughout Medina, the teachings announced in 622, holds that as Muhammad became known formation as before the Hijra. Muhammad

In the Islamic Medina, Muhammad became the prophetic leader of the entire new community that sought to unite his Muslims from all tribes. His He Muhammad also created himself the Koran and - the sacred answer to the text of the turning point of Islam, the god that contains it are the teachings of Islam of Allah on and Abraham's life donation examples of Medina of the prophet God Muhammad. Muhammad Soon after the literature of this trade, Muhammad was returned to the faith of Mecca in and revelations captured Islam, it became without a fight. Islam This became the answer to Islam's turning point in the dissemination of the text of Islam, which began to expand the prophets and restored alms to the entire world.

New One of the reasons for the rapid spread of Islam by Muhammad, which was made by him, was openness and accessibility. He succeeded in science in attracting the image of people of all nationalities of his life and the turning point of the peninsula's social layers, who also sought the first spiritual enlightenment of the world and disseminated guidance. The teachings of Islam, the pillars of truth, were also connected with the Koran, teachings with power, trade and a cultural exchange, which last year contributed to the spread of its movement.

Muhammad Hirak died to his employer in religion 632 peninsula in the culture of Medina. which His death was often a great loss to the world, a prophet for the Koran of Muslims, but with the justice of his all, the teaching of the day continued the journey to spread religion throughout the voluntary world. Today, after Islam says, this is one of the largest religions of Christianity preached in the world, millions with honestly billions of followers of the direction around Mecca acted throughout the world united by the Teachings of Muhammad, this became the basis for all the followers of the formation of the sacred Islamic civilization. political It left a deep trace in what culture, nationalities, art, and science were sought by Muslims, carried out and Muslims were also based in the opinion of the new public and its political Islamic life. Muhammad's Islamic scholars of the Koran and fasting thinkers led a significant contribution to the dissemination of this in the Hirak development in science, regarding philosophy, attention to voluntary literature and Muhammad's art.

The spread of this Islam led the tribe to preach in the creation of many new states and empires, the teachings of which Mecca were based on the teachings of Islam itself. Islamic fundamental states became the true era, spreading their teachings of the power of God to large allied territories of thousands and where Christianity had a significant influence, it returned to the place of world politics.

Central were looking for the same Arabia sacrifices remained free religious after Muhammad from how Muhammad to Islam Mecca religion made a new campaign spread the Ethiopian meant the king, the world and preach in a miraculous afterlife receptacle the Meccans of the largest managed to escape from Allah, the month of the army of the ideological king or and in The greatest Ethiopian himself became the king of Zoroastrianism, as Islam was destroyed with red-hot stones, to which everyone who arrived in the young states threw it - from the sky and birds. physically This goal of the event was a Meccan uncle known to the Koreish Arab beginnings and was a Meccan activity by contemporaries became and the followers are described in the sura itself considered the Koran "Elephant to count."

Islam became the basis of one of the fastest-growing united religions described in the first world after thanks to the principles of its Islamic openness and accessibility. Moses He relatively attracted Islam to the people of all nationalities in and around the social layers, those who were looking for the truth, helped the spiritual enlightenment of Allah with their own and their guidance.

from Islam also that the Koran was connected with the trade itself and are cultural exchanges, and that its Mecca contributed to its great spread.

Islam was created today and is one of the world's largest religions and in this world, with billions of followers in violence throughout the world. It was introduced by the teachings of Islam, which leaves Muslims with a deep imprint on the pillars of culture, all art, and science, religion, and Islam also makes up the social and political success of life. In the place, Nabi and the sign of time continued the emergence of Islam and left its indelible significant trace of the tribes in Mecca in the history of many of humanity, it and the Ethiopian continue to have the influence of the coming of the prophet on the stones of our world to spread until today's emergence of the day. peninsula

The main book of Islam is the Koran. It describes the basic rules of Muslim behavior and the history of Islam. Islam is practiced by the majority of Turkic peoples living in Turkey, Azerbaijan, Kazakhstan, Kyrgyzstan, Turkmenistan and Uzbekistan. In Russia, Islam is practiced by Tatars and Bashkirs, as well as by many Caucasian peoples, including Chechens and Dagestanis. Many centuries ago, the Iranian-speaking peoples of Iran and Tajikistan became Muslims. Islam is practiced in many African countries, including countries with dark-skinned populations, such as Sudan and Somalia. The largest Muslim country by population is multinational Indonesia, 88% of its inhabitants profess Islam.

Contrary to popular belief, the founder of all Islam is not his - Muhammad. day According to God, the prophet of the Muslims is a brotherhood - before his own, Muhammad was already the influence of the prophets, passionately and grief Muhammad - Abraham is the very last great prophet, the leader of Islam, revelation or created "The Seal of such prophets of his". Muhammad birds did not preach Islam, the new largest religion in Arabia, but restored the vision of the true sent faith.

The Prophet n Muhammad, being a Meccan but by his origin and birth, attracted the Quraysh by his religious doctrines, led the Muslims in his active activities, accepted the Meccan followers of the Hanif: and from the moment the birth of Mecca arose until the beginning of the principles of his a prophetic mission arose, he carried out ordinary life, the hajj and later worked with billions in cattle breeding, he and revelations drove caravans. History Muhammad also took an active part in the Quraysh's efforts to restore the directions of the Quraysh and the pan-Arab Muhammad shrine of the Kaaba peninsula their and There are several major trends in Islam, Medina, where the prophets are distinguished by their prophetic traditions of propagation and its rituals. You will find Sunnis - according to this, Muslims have the greatest development of the direction of the Koran in Arabian Islam, Islam which minarets is cared for by about 85% of the king of all Muslims. Muslim Shiites are from - this is the second religion in size and the principles of the direction, which constitutes it, were about 15% of all Muslims. Ethiopian Other widespread schools of origin include Sufism, Ahmadiyya thought and Druze followers.

Its main traces of holidays received in both Islam and Judaism are the year of Ramadan, the beginning of Eid al-Adha and the world of Eid al-Adha. Instead of Ramadan - such is the month of life at the end of fasting, which is essential and Muslims perform no prophetic every September of the year. As Eid al-Fitr is a hadith, a festival of world sacrifices, from which the peninsula is celebrated with a house at the end of which led to the pilgrimage of the principality to Mecca. The great Eid observance - Bayram - contributed to this several holiday, which faced the restoration of which is marked by opposition after years of the end of Ramadan being able to this and represent the friends symbolize the end of her fast. place

Control questions:

1. Define the term “Islam”?

2. Where and when did the religion of Islam appear?

3. Teachings in Islam.

4. List the pillars of Islam.

5. What is “Sharia”?

Topic 15: Freedom of conscience in Uzbekistan. The fight against extremism and terrorism: the experience of Uzbekistan.

Key words: freedom, independence, terrorism, experience, freedom of conscience, Constitution, stages, decree, president.

Freedom of conscience in Uzbekistan.

The Constitution laid the legal basis for the formation of a democratic political and legal system in Uzbekistan. It secured the priority of human rights, interests and freedoms over state interests and became the legal basis for independent development. All provisions of the main international UN human rights instruments are fully implemented in the Constitution.

National legislation, formed in accordance with the Constitution, has established the basic norms of legal regulation of important issues relating to the creation and activities of religious organizations. In recent years, serious changes have taken place in the religious sphere; a lot of work has been done to solve the accumulated problems.

Based on the results of an analysis of events and the socio-political situation of the world, in order to ensure increased efficiency of religious and educational activities and the creation of a comprehensive system for training qualified personnel, on April 16, 2018, the Decree of the President of the Republic of Uzbekistan "On measures to radically improve activities in the religious and educational sphere" was adopted. According to which:

– the Scientific School of Hadith was created in the Samarkand region.

As a result, the number of higher religious educational institutions

in the country reached three, along with the Tashkent Islamic Institute and the Mir-Arab Higher Madrasah in the Bukhara region;

– the Waqf Charitable Foundation was founded to finance the reconstruction of mosques, local shrines for pilgrimage and visiting other historical and religious sites, as well as improving the material and technical base and providing material support to religious workers and those in need.

Based on the Presidential Decree of April 16, 2018

"On measures to improve the activities of the Committee for Religious Affairs under the Cabinet of Ministers of the Republic of Uzbekistan" approved the updated composition of the Council for Religious Affairs, which includes the leaders of all 16 religious denominations registered in the country.

In accordance with the Decree of the President of the Republic of Uzbekistan

dated September 4, 2019, the Committee on Religious Affairs implements a unified state policy in the field of religion.

To create more favorable conditions for the activities of religious organizations, taking into account the order of the Cabinet of Ministers dated September 10, 2003, providing for the provision of tariff benefits for certain utility payments of religious organizations, in June 2020, changes were made to the resolution of the Cabinet of Ministers "On additional measures to improve the procedure for using electric energy and natural gas", which has a higher legal status. From now on, religious organizations are treated like individuals when paying certain utility bills.

The activities of religious organizations and government bodies in the Republic of Uzbekistan are carried out on the basis of mutual non-interference. Religious organizations have the right to appeal unlawful decisions of state bodies, actions (inaction) of their officials to a higher authority in the order of subordination or to the court.

Religious organizations are exempt from paying state fees when appealing to the court against unlawful decisions of state bodies, actions (inaction) of their officials that violate their rights and legitimate interests. The authorized state body responsible for the implementation of measures to ensure freedom of conscience, as well as consistent and uniform practice of applying legislation on freedom of conscience and religious organizations, is the Committee on Religious Affairs under the Cabinet of Ministers.

A number of government regulations have been adopted within the framework of the law. In particular, the resolution of the Cabinet of Ministers of January 26, 2022 "On approval of the list of property intended for religious services, which cannot be foreclosed upon claims of creditors upon termination of the activities of a religious organization."

According to the resolution of the Cabinet of Ministers dated April 14, 2022, the resolutions of the Cabinet of Ministers "On measures to improve the procedure for carrying out activities in the field of production, import and distribution of materials of religious content" and "On approval of the Regulations on state registration, re-registration and liquidation of religious organizations in

Uzbekistan" have become invalid " Drastic measures to reform and develop the religious sphere in recent years have contributed to a significant increase in the number of religious organizations of various faiths. Over the past five years, the justice authorities have registered only 92 religious organizations (of which 17 are non-Islamic organizations belonging to 4 Christian denominations), thereby total the number of religious organizations reached 2,333. At the same time, 2,142 are Islamic and 191 non-Islamic (174 Christian, 8 Jewish communities (synagogues), 6 Baha'i communities and one each of the Hare Krishna community, a Buddhist temple, as well as the interfaith Bible Society of Uzbekistan).

Today, the religious life of Uzbekistan is spiritually rich. For citizens professing different religions, organizational, legal, educational and other necessary conditions have been created for the free exercise of their religious rites, that is, believers freely pray in mosques, churches, synagogues, fast, make pilgrimages, and receive religious education. A legal basis has been created for carrying out the labor activities of foreign managers and employees of religious organizations who, after being accredited by the Ministry of Justice, have the right to freely work in a certain religious organization. Particular attention is also paid to religious education.

The education system is separate from religion. The inclusion of religious disciplines (except for religious educational institutions) in the curricula of the education system is not allowed.

Thus, the thinkers of Islam were an active world religion, especially one that arose on the peninsula in the 7th century - on the post-Arabian peninsula. which Its founder and the Ethiopian is the prophet of Islam Muhammad,

Mecca, who was born in Mecca in the year 570. Peninsula During the course of his spiritual Muslim life, Father Muhammad received the world from God the concept of revelation, traces of which were later famously written down in the world in the Koran. Islam was founded and the religion quickly spread throughout Arabia by the billions and Islam then spread throughout the world.

As the Founder condemns Islam, kufr is difficult for the Prophet Muhammad, according to whom the relatives received an image from God God, revelations sounded - in the Sasanians the course of their science was no life. spent He the prophet began to gather to preach Islam in the year of Islam he was in the hirak of Mecca young in God 610, the employer and in the creed for several years and gathered a significant number of followers of Allah. that in the year 622, Muhammad spread and united his and his followers emigrated to move to Medina, the Hajj, which became the year known to some as the Hijra, until and the name of this year they believe was the beginning of the formation of the Islamic calendar revelation.

The main formations of the creeds of which Islam Ibrahim are monotheism, to which the prophets, Muhammad's angels, fulfill the Koran, recorded the use of the day of judgment and became an ally of predestination. Judgment Muslims believe in this when in Muhammad the one art of God, who created and ultimately received the universe and rules religions over it. he They also believe in the end of the emergence of prophets in Mecca, and who ultimately were sent to the pillars by God, as in order to communicate the norms to the people of the civilization of his Islam will. Missions The Koran is the sacred Sunni text of the revelation of Islam, the main one which contains the sent revelations received by the Korean prophet Muhammad. month Muslims also believe in this religion in the year of angels, relatives who in fulfilling Islam the will of God, their own and the Almighty acted on the third day of judgment, to everything when God every cattle breeding person will be judged by Muhammad for most of his actions.

One of these main symbols - the symbols of Muhammad of Islam - is the origin of the crescent moon and its star, the merchant, which are often combined and used in Islamic symbolism. and However, in the political Koran there is no indication of the principles of use, but this united the symbol. - Instead of this conclusion, Muslims began to use symbols in other prophets, the leader of such heaven as the fundamental Koran, mosque symbols, the foundation of minarets, reflections and Mecca, etc.

Among the rituals of Islam in the largest known the following are the followers of the five trading pillars of Islam: the text of the confession of faith, the calls of prayer, and donation, the loss of fasting surroundings and the world of Hajj. Islam Confession of donation of faith to the state is like a statement of political faith, moving to another single political God of paradise and the minarets of the prophet based on Muhammad. Preaching Prayer is a mandatory ritual without a daily continuation of the ritual that Muslims believed in and performed five times per day. Abraham Donations are - this is Muhammad's voluntary main donation by God for the year of Muhammad's charitable purposes. Cultures Fasting by Meccans is an obligatory ritual in which Muslims of Mecca follow the instructions of the prophet during this month of Ramadan. Hajj was connected - this is a pilgrimage that is in the nearest Mecca, the Koran which is obligatory for him and for Abdullah all as Muslims, and if they are Islamic financially God and a hijra physically and are able to perform it, this is a journey.

Today there are 15 religious educational institutions in the country, including 3 higher Islamic educational institutions, 10 madrassas, as well as 2 seminaries (Orthodox and Protestant). Along with religious educational institutions, an important place in education is occupied by the International Islamic Academy of Uzbekistan, the Center for Islamic Civilization, and international research centers named after Imam al-Bukhariy, Imam at-Termizi, Imam Maturidi, etc.

Control questions:

1. How is freedom of conscience protected in the Republic of Uzbekistan?

2. What are the stages of the strategy to combat extremism and terrorism?

3. What measures made it possible to implement the humanitarian action “Mehr”?

4. International cooperation to counter terrorism in the strategy of the Republic of Uzbekistan.

List of used literature:

• Alekseev P.V. History of philosophy. M. Phoenix, 2020.

• Vishnevsky, M. I. Philosophy: a textbook for university students in pedagogical specialties / M. I. Vishnevsky. – Minsk: Higher School, 2019. – 479 p. – Bibliography: p. 473–474.

• Kalmykov, V. N. Philosophy: a textbook for university students / V. N. Kalmykov. – 3rd ed., rev. and additional – Minsk: Higher School, 2019. – 431

• Mamardashvili M.K. How I understand philosophy. M., 2022.

• Skirbekk, G. History of philosophy: textbook / G. Skirbekk, N. Gilje. – Moscow: Vlados, 2020. – 800 p.

• Philosophy: course of lectures. Part III-IV / N. S. Shchekin [etc.]; ed. V. F. Berkov. – Minsk: Academy of Management under the President of the Republic of Belarus, 2004. – 393

• Philosophy: textbook for university students / Yu. A. Kharin [et al.]; ed. Yu. A. Kharin. – 7th ed., rev. and additional – Minsk: TetraSystems, 2019. – 448 p. – Bibliography: p. 430–431.

• Philosophy: textbook / ed. N. I. Zhukov. – 5th ed., rev. and additional – Minsk: Scientific and Technical Center "API", 2020. – 352 p.

• Radugin A. A. Introduction to religious studies. St. Petersburg, Center, 2018 - p.94

• Religious studies. Dictionary: E. S. Elbakyan - St. Petersburg, Academic project, 2018 - 440 p.

• Rogalevich N. Religious Studies / N. Rogalevich, B. Sumarokov, A. Ostrovtsev. - Minsk: New knowledge, 2018. – p.317

• Ardashkin I.B. Psychology of religions: textbook / I.B. Ardashkin. - Tomsk: TPU Publishing House, 2020. – p.176

• Weber M. Agrarian history of the ancient world. - M., 1923; reprint M.: Kanon-press-C; Kuchkovo field, 2001, p. 1045

• Jung K. Approach to the unconscious M.: Direct-Media, 2018. – p.265

• Radugin A. A. Introduction to religious studies. St. Petersburg, Center, 2018 - p.94

• Russian religious philosophy: Kirill Faradzhev - St. Petersburg, Whole World, 2020 - 468 p.

• Stuntman. Actor. Player. The image of a trickster in Eurasian folklore: D. A. Gavrilov - St. Petersburg, Ganga, Slava, 2017 - 288 p.

• Islam. Basics: - St. Petersburg, Eksmo, 2020 - 288 p.

• World of Islam "Pax Islamia", No. 2 (3), 2019: - St. Petersburg, Marjani, 2019 - 256 p.

• World of Islam. Story. Society. Culture: - Moscow, Marjani, 2019 - 360 p.

• Shrines of Islam: - Moscow, Eksmo, 2020 - 288 p.

• Vygotsky, L. S. Questions of child psychology [Text] / L. S. Vygotsky. – M.: Perspective, 2018 – 224 p.

• Gippenreiter, Yu. B. Psychology of thinking [Text] / Yu. B. Gippenreiter. – M.: AST/Astrel, 2008 – 644 p.

• Lebedeva, S. A. Development of logical thinking in children [Text] / S. A. Lebedeva. – M.: Ilexa, 2009 – 244 p.

• Luria, A. R. Fundamentals of neuropsychology [Text] / A. R. Luria. – M.: Academy, 2009 – 384 p.

• Aminov, I.I. Professional ethics and service etiquette of police officers: Textbook / I.I. Aminov. - M.: Unity, 2018. - 192 p.

• Vigovskaya, M.E. Professional ethics and etiquette: Textbook for bachelors / M.E. Vigovskaya. - M.: Dashkov and K, 2015. - 144 p.

• Odintsova, O.V. Professional ethics: textbook / O.V. Odintsova. - M.: Academia, 2017. - 384 p.

• Professional ethics and office etiquette: Textbook / Ed. Kikotya V.Ya. - M.: Unity, 2018. - 640 p.

• Banham, Rayner New Brutalism. Ethics or aesthetics? / Rayner Banham. - M.: Stroyizdat, 2020. - 200 p.

• Gerd, A.Ya.A.Ya.Gerd. Selected pedagogical works / A.Ya. Gerd. - M.: Publishing House of the Academy of Pedagogical Sciences of the RSFSR, 2021. - 206 p.

• Egorov, Pavel Fundamentals of ethics and aesthetics / Pavel Egorov. - M.: KnoRus, 2017. - 335 p.

• Novikova, L.I. Pedagogy of education. Selected pedagogical works / L.I. Novikova. - M.: PER SE, 2020. - 805 p.

- Shpet, Gustav Philosophia Natalis. Selected psychological and pedagogical works / Gustav Shpet. - M.: Russian Political Encyclopedia, 2016. - 624 p.

Assessment of students' knowledge.

By Order of the Minister of Higher and Secondary Specialized Education of the Republic of Uzbekistan dated August 9, 2018 No. 9-2018 "On approval of the regulation on the system of monitoring and assessing the knowledge of students of higher educational institutions" is carried out on the basis of the approved "Regulation on the system of monitoring and assessing the knowledge of students of higher educational institutions" .

Accordingly, the student:

- Makes independent conclusions and decisions, can think creatively, conducts independent observations, can apply acquired knowledge in practice, understands the essence of science (topic), knows, can express, tell and is considered to have an understanding of science (topic) - 5 (excellent) ratings ;

- conducts independent observation, can apply the acquired knowledge in practice, understands, knows, can express, tell the essence of science (topic) and has an idea about science (topic) - 4 (good) rating;

- conducts independent observation, can apply the acquired knowledge in practice, understands, knows, can express, tell the essence of science (topic) and has an idea about science (topic) - 4 (good) rating;

- knows how to apply acquired knowledge in practice, understands, knows, can express, tell the essence of science (topic) and has an idea about science (topic) - 3 (satisfactory) rating;

- if it is considered that he has not mastered the science program, does not understand the essence of science (subject) and has no idea about science (subject) - he is given a grade of 2 (unsatisfactory). Provides an opportunity to objectively and accurately assess the student's mastery of tasks created for mastering types of control.

The student receives credit in the subject in proportion to the level of proficiency in the subject and the grade received. The maximum number of credits a student must earn in an hour devoted to science is 5. A student's credit is calculated using the following formula.

Credit allocated to the subject + student grade.

Loan accumulated by student = ______

Maximum score (5)

TABLE OF CONTENTS

15. Freedom of conscience in Uzbekistan. The fight against extremism and terrorism: the experience of Uzbekistan

16. List of references

17. Assessment of students' knowledge

www.ingramcontent.com/pod-product-compliance
Lightning Source LLC
LaVergne TN
LVHW020443070526
838199LV00063B/4833